Spiritu Lives of (Adolescents: Some Perspectives

Edited by

Marian de Souza
and
Winifred Wing Han Lamb

ATF Press
Adelaide

Spirituality in the Lives of Children and Adolescents: Some Perspectives

Contents

Editorial

Marian de Souza
Ballarat
Winifred Wing Ham Lamb
Canberra

In the contemporary Western world that is permeated with materialistic values and consumerist inclinations, there has emerged, almost in counterpoint, a deep and abiding interest in spirituality. This began at the end of the twentieth century as a grass roots movement when many, disenchanted with traditional religious institutions began to search for meaning along alternate pathways. One symptom of the movement was the flourishing of the New Age movement and its associated paraphernalia such as publications, objects, markets, exhibitions and, indeed, lifestyles. As well, there has been a trend for some to turn to different faith groups so that Buddhism and conservative Christian groups have begun to grow in numbers in some western countries. At another level, there is some evidence that fundamentalism is on the rise which may be an attempt by some religious and political leaders to establish a stronger foothold, regain some ground and exert some control on their diminishing communities.[1]

Another sign of the times is the accelerating interest in spirituality (as distinct from religion and religiosity[2]) as a

---

1. See Stephen Law argument that conservative thinking is attempting to overtake liberalism in *The War for Children's Minds* (Abingdon, Oxford: Routledge, 2006).
2. Hannegraaff offers some relevant discussion on this distinction in his article, WJ Hanegraaff, 'New Age spiritualities as Secular Religion: A

serious study and insights on spirituality have been adopted by diverse fields of study, including medicine and health; psychology, social work and sociology; education and pastoral care. Alongside this has emerged an extended understanding about the role of spirituality in the lives and wellbeing of children and adolescents.

Over the past few years, studies of children and adolescents has led to the conclusion that factors such as a sense of belonging, belief in self and other, hope and resilience should be nurtured and promoted amongst children and young people.[3] It is generally agreed that these positive traits can counter negative ones like hopelessness and despair, violence to self and others, alienation and marginalisation. What is pertinent here is that some contemporary understandings of spirituality describe it as pertaining to the relational dimension of being, the connectedness that an individual experiences to Self and to Other in the human and non-human world.[4] Certainly, many professionals working with the young, particularly in the areas of health and education, have begun to explore and espouse new understandings of spirituality and its

---

Historian's Perspective', *Social Compass*, Volume 46, Number 2, (1999): 145–60.

3.   For instance, see the report from the Commission on Children at Risk, US, *Hardwired to Connect: The scientific Case for Authoritative Communities* at <http://www.americanvalues.org/html/hardwired_-_ex_ summary.html>. Accessed 3 November 2003.
     As well, see A Fuller; G Johnson; B Bellhouse and K McGraw, *START: School Transition and Resilience Training*, (Victoria, Australia: Department of Education and Training, 2003) or Richard Eckersley's discussion in *Well and Good: How We Feel and Why it Matters* (Australia: The Text Publishing Company, 2003). All these make some reference, explicitly or implicitly, to connectedness and belonging as being crucial factors in children's wellbeing.
4.   In particular, see Rebecca Nye's description of relational consciousness in David Hay and Rebecca Nye, *The Spirit of the Child* (London: Fount Paperbacks, 1998).

role in human life. In addition, attempts have been made to identify specific ways in which spirituality may be addressed and nurtured so as to increase and enhance the wellbeing of our children and young people through educational and other programs.

The perspective on spirituality described above is foundational to some of the articles within this issue and various studies and research have provided the basis for the topics that are featured. To begin with, there is some discussion of childhood. However, the notion of childhood is a contentious one. Recent controversial reports like *Corporate Paedophilia: Sexualisation of children in Australia* published by the Australia Institute[5] reflect an aspect of the debate around the affluent world. The expressed concerns correlate to a range of claims, such as that children need protection from exploitation by advertising and marketing and that depictions of children in such media involve a loss of innocence. At the same time, it is suggested that children are propelled too quickly into the role of consumer, that they are given too much in the way of material goods. On the other hand, there are those who point out that in affluent child-centred cultures children are given too much protection and focus, to the point of 'idolisation'.[6]

The context of the debate matters. So too, the values which frame our notion of the child. If we can resist taking the child as an 'idol' that reflects our own needs and expectations, s/he can speak to us as an 'icon'. Anthony Kelly's paper presents this challenge as he takes the discussion outside the context of 'the contractual and rights-oriented conceptions' of contemporary debate, to focus on the child as 'saturated phenomenon'. He argues that far from embodying 'a stage that is to be left

5. E Rush and A La Nauze, *Corporate Paedophilia: Sexualisation of Children in Australia*, Australia Institute, Discussion Paper # 90, 2006.
6. D Donahoo, *Idolising Children* (Sydney: University of New South Wales Press, 2007).

behind' the child carries a prophetic power to call us to account. S/he is a 'unique revelation', a 'gift incarnate', a 'event' that faces us with important questions about our 'shared world and the deeper reaches of its meaning.' Above all, s/he points to the heart of God whose favour rests 'to a surprising degree with "the little ones" that are invisible in the harsh demands of social life.'

Joyce Mercer's discussion of 'boredom' gives us a window into the lives of children in affluent contemporary societies. She points out that the experience and characterisation of 'boredom' as a judgment of a situation 'demanding correction by others' is a relatively recent notion. While its earlier cousins such as the medieval concept of *acedia* (or sloth) was understood to be the responsibility of the bearer, boredom is now seen as being located outside the sufferer to which he or she falls victim. Mercer argues that the 'normalisation' of boredom shows that consumerism has indeed become a dominating paradigm in as far as boredom reflects the expectation for novelty at every turn and the quest for 'intense experiences and "spectacle" in every day life'. The self as consumer and client must be satisfied. The implications for psychological and spiritual development are plain. Mercer suggests that the challenge for parents and teachers is to empower children with an 'alternative vocabulary for naming the experiences they (and we) currently classify as boredom' to resist the power of market culture over their lives and to make room for spiritual development.

Glen Cupit echoes Mercer's concerns when he discusses the impact of electronic media on the spiritual development of the child. Cupit reflects on the importance of narrative in nurturing spirituality especially in earlier times when these narratives were handed down through an oral tradition which helped a new generation understand and interact with their world. In the modern world, children access narratives through the electronic media which is difficult for adults to monitor. Cupit urges his reader to recognise the impact of this new genre of narrative on children's spirituality. He acknowledges that in the past, the Christian world was influenced by the biblical understanding of children as lacking in moral judgment, in reason, understanding and in clear expression. Furthermore, they were seen as vulnerable and needing protection from negative influences, such as heathen idols. Whilst Cupit acknowledges that it is 'a long step' from heathen idols to secular television, there are some aspects of television programming that can 'impoverish, darken and oppress the human spirit'. Further, they may convey messages and sentiments that are instrumental in damaging the relationship of the individual with God. As Cupit points out it is difficult to arrive at the truth if the ways of society are focused on 'misrepresenting reality'. A significant element in Cupit's discussion is the need to allow children to have exposure to narratives that both positively nurture spirituality but also those which detract from spiritual development. In the latter instance, there is a need to help children become discerning so that they are able to exercise judgment about the messages they are receiving. This is a more effective way of preparing them to live and be in their worlds as spiritual people.

Yet another perspective is offered by Jerome Berryman who discusses the difficulties that we have when speaking of and teaching about evil. This could be described as the shadow side of human relationality and it is something that many children experience and have questions about. However, Berryman argues that most teachers and other significant adults in the lives of children do not handle the topic of evil competently. He then proceeds to offer pertinent insights into why this occurs and to offers some suggestions, including the use of narrative and language, for teachers to assist in teaching children about evil.

Another perspective from Anne Hunt challenges, not only the conventional view of children's wisdom and spirituality but also their spiritual stature. Her account of the childhood of saints and mystics shows the capacity of children for profound experiences and early vocation, their ability to lead rigorously holy lives and their extraordinary depth of devotion. For example, from an early age, Therese of Lisieux 'experienced an intense desire to suffer for God' and claimed that from the age of three years, she never refused God anything. These lives 'inundated by grace' and 'personal encounter with the divine mystery' can interrogate adult sensibilities about children and their capacities.

The final two articles explore aspects of spirituality in education. Drawing on his own research, Brendan Hyde discusses children's spirituality through three key concepts: 'ultimate unity', 'universal consciousness' and the 'collective self'. The essence of each of these concepts is the acknowledgment of the presence of the divine as a unifying element at the core of each individual which may lead him/her to the experience of becoming one with other. Hyde illustrates aspects of this notion, in particular to the concept of the 'collective self', through descriptions of various activities that were undertaken with primary school children and offers guidelines to religious education teachers to nurture the spirituality of their students.

Extending this, Marian de Souza defines spirituality broadly as the 'expression of the relational dimensions of the individual' and as 'deep connection of 'inner' and 'outer self' as well as 'self' with 'other'. She then discusses how such experiences may be recognised and fostered within education and focuses on the element of intuition which is optimised in the sense of 'flow'. Phenomenologically, the individual experiences a state in which their consciousness is harmoniously ordered. De Souza recommends that school curriculum should focus on 'educating' the intuitions of students with programmes and pedagogy which engage them more holistically to promote synoptic and deep understanding.

With their focus on both 'children' and 'spirituality', the articles in this issue are a window on the contemporary world, reflecting a diversity of views on the nature of the self, of human flourishing and of the transcendent.

Spirituality and the Child

Anthony J Kelly
Melbourne

It is often remarked that exploitative pressures of the modern consumer society have the effect of robbing the child of childhood (to say nothing of robbing parents of parenthood). The fear is that the imagination of children can be so colonised by diseased cultural forces that they are increasingly forced into being 'little adults'. They must grow up before their time, exposed to the erotic and consumerist propensities of the culture they breathe. This volume addresses many concerns in this area. In this brief essay, rather than pretending to comment on the spirituality of children themselves, I wish to focus on the spiritual significance of the child for the world of adults.[1] What follows presents first a brief remark on the multi-dimensional phenomenon of the child, and then moves on to a biblical reflection on the witness of the child.

1. The manifold phenomenon of the child

Genuine phenomenological methods seek to escape the self-referential and projective mechanisms of dominant ideologies. Attention to the phenomenon counteracts abstract generalisations and principles, in order to appreciate what is actually 'given' in the unobjectifiable particularity of experience.[2]

---

1. See Robert K Vischer, 'The Best Interests of the Child: Modern Lessons from Christian Traditions', in the forthcoming *The Vocation of the Child,* edited by Patrick Brennan (Grand Rapids: Eerdmans, 2007).

2. Jean-Luc Marion, *In Excess: Studies of Saturated Phenomena,* translated by Robyn Horner and Vincent Barraud (New York: Fordham University Press, 2002), 1–29.

Neither philosophical nor theological thinking begins or ends with abstract ideas in a theoretical world. Nor does it inspect 'data' in a neutral, dispassionate sense. In naming and exploring the human, genuine thinking is characterised by receptivity to the unique reality of particular persons in a social world of communication. To the Christian vision, indeed, each human being is a God-defined mystery, created, called and redeemed by an original and ultimate love.

In this phenomenological perspective, a distinction given currency by Jean-Luc Marion proves useful. The child is not to be taken as an 'idol', reflecting back to society our own needs and expectations, but, rather, as an 'icon' through which the light of larger reality shines through, in its originality and provocative 'otherness'.[3] Marion in his later writings appeals to 'saturated phenomena' of different kinds. However odd-sounding this phrase is in English, it refers to particular phenomena that overbrim with significance, such as a world-forming event or a great work of art—and others that he names as 'revelation', 'the flesh', and 'the face'.[4] Though some have reproached him for transgressing the limits of philosophy by appealing to theological considerations, we are not here concerned with such academic distinctions. Our concern is to attend to the phenomenon, the particularly 'saturated' phenomenon, of the child. Inspired by his approach, I will focus on the phenomenon of the child, as it 'saturates' our capacities to think about our shared world and the deeper reaches of its meaning: 'Unto us a son is given', as Handel's oratorio has it

3. See Jean-Luc Marion, *God Without Being*, translated by Thomas A Carlson (Chicago: University of Chicago Press, 1991), 12–16, 29–30, 69.

4. See especially Marion, *In Excess*, 30–102, and *Being Given: Toward a Phenomenology of Givenness*, translated by Jeffrey L Kosky (Stanford: Stanford University Press, 2002), 235–6. For a discerning theological commentary, Robyn Horner, *Jean-Luc Marion: A Theo-logical Introduction* (Burlington: Ashgate Publishing, 2005), 103–50.

(see Isa 9:6). In the birth of a child, life is taken to a new frontier: to the limit to present experience, and a further limit of what is coming to be.

First of all, the child comes in the form of a unique 'revelation'. It[5] breaks into the experience as the occurrence of the new, at once a gift and a promise given into the heart of life. The child is in this way the focus of wonder at the generativity of the universe disclosed in this way. She calls the whole human family to a new responsibility, if parents and relatives are to receive this gift of a new beginning in reverence and care. The child, therefore, embodies a question: What new thing is being given, being revealed? What creative source, what ultimate giver, what guiding providence is involved as revealed in this gift?

Secondly, the child is an 'event'. Despite the vulnerability of both the child and his mother, the event or advent of a child has the power to affect all it touches. The arrival of a child evokes a new sense of both the immemorial generations of the past and of the undetermined future. The birth of a child is in this way an open-ended, transformative event. It is no *fait accompli* in terms of assignable causes and predictable effects, but an advent whose significance overflows as a unique new presence within the constitution of family, society and even world-history. To this degree, it is in the nature of such an event to resist calculated prediction of outcomes, but to inspire waiting, fidelity and hope, if what is given is to be received in its incalculable significance. The child-as-event poses a question: what generative happening has taken place? How will it overflow into the existence of parents, family, society, the world? How will this gift be played out in the all-encompassing event of creation itself?

---

5.   I recognise that 'it' is not the right pronoun, since every child is 'he' or 'she'. For our purposes, I will vary the pronoun for the sake of greater inclusiveness: I hope this will not be too confusing.

Thirdly, it is a gift and event, incarnate—in the 'flesh' of human life. This embodiment can, of course, be analysed in terms of genetics and biology; but, more than being an instance of natural animal offspring, the child is en-fleshed, incarnate, in a world of human, embodied persons. Born out of intimate union of its parents who have come together in the flesh, the child is conceived as an irreducible 'other', handed over to their care. Despite the possibilities of violence and exploitation inherent in a grossly sexual objectification of relationships, the child is a witness to something else. He embodies, within the intimacy, ecstasy and generativity of our incarnate existence, a distinctively personal order of relationships. For she implicitly demands to be received as something more than a biological product of two sexual agents, and so to provoke a larger sense of life. As an incarnate gift, event and revelation, the child poses further questions: what is this larger sense of life? What mystery of life does it point to? How, in the Christian phenomenology of life centred in the Incarnation, is the child related to the Word made flesh, given into the world from the eternal generativity of God himself? Parents are more than agents of biological procreation, and their child is more than either a designed product—or unwanted by-product—of their union.

Fourthly, the phenomenon of the child occurs with something of the impact of a 'work of art'. All great art resists any one-dimensional approach. In the case of great painting, for example, the beholder or succession of beholders are never confined to one point of view. What is depicted resists containment; it overflows any one perception. Such a work may be an object in the art-market, and even reduced to a feature of interior design or decoration. But, of its nature, it never fits in to a pre-designed space: its power is to command its own space and change the place given it. The phenomenon of art can be analogically related to the phenomenon of the child, even if she is not 'artistically' mproduced by human agency. We can say, without indulging in sentimentality, that the child is 'given' as embodying a revelation of the wonder and luminous tenderness of being. As Francis Webb in a well-known poem, 'Five Days Old', writes,

> The tiny, not the immense,
> will teach our groping eyes.
> So the absorbed skies
> bleed stars of innocence.
>
> ....
>
> Now wonderingly engrossed
> In your fearless delicacies,
> I am launched upon sacred seas,
> Humbly and utterly lost
> In the mystery of creation . . . [6]

There is further point to the poet's words. Despite her vulnerability, like the impact of the beautiful, the child is a disruption. He is not given to 'fit in', as a technical production. She calls for a new vision, and reconciliation among those whose murderous demands have foreclosed on new possibilities and made the world a dangerous place for children. The gospels present the Christ child lying in the manger as both hymned by the angels and discovered by the lowly shepherds, while the imperial world was engaged in a census. Webb concludes his poem:

> If this is man, then the danger
> And fear are as lights of the inn,
> Faint and remote as sin

---

6.   Francis Webb, 'Five Days Old', in Kevin Hart (introduction and editor), *The Oxford Book of Australian Religious Verse* (Oxford and New York: Oxford University Press, 1994), 225.

Out there by the manger.
In the sleeping, weeping weather
We shall all kneel down together.

Lastly, the presence of the child can be viewed in terms of the saturated phenomenon of 'the face'. The face of the other is not a projection on one's part of the other as an object, useful, exploitable or ignored, as the case might be. It stands for the totality of the reality of the other as given, calling me to responsibility. To allow oneself to be 'faced' by the other in this way, is to be called out of oneself, to make room for this other, however unsettling this may prove. In the child, society and culture are faced with fresh responsibility and care. The tears of a child demand an assurance that all is well—ultimately—and even now—in as much making all to be well is our present responsibility. Once more, the question: in the name of what do we respond to the child and assure him of hope, and promise a peace that will not betray her?

These five aspects of the phenomenon of the child as 'saturating' our perceptions of self, the world and its ultimate mysteries, will hardly coincide with the strange notions of the 'right-to-be wanted-child' of today. Past anxieties of 'another mouth to feed' are reissued in the cultural version of the 'wanted' child of today. To repeat, these aspects as I have presented them bear not so much on a child's spirituality, but on the character of the spirituality of the culture and society into which he is born: what does the child calls us to, and what is demanded of the various communities that affect her? Each of these aspects occupies a limit—either negatively, of a limit beyond which the culture will not go; or, more positively, the limit of a region of love and care in which this vulnerable other will be safe. The more one moves into this realm of responsibility, the more deeply philosophical and religious considerations stir.[7] Does the child call us to a sense in which we are all 'children of the universe'—and more ultimately, 'children of God'? Is the child simply there in an extreme of vulnerability, or the incarnate symbol of our common contingency in the universe, and of the hopes that a generative, healing love is at its heart?[8] Does the phenomenon of the child approached in these ways call the society and church itself into a new kind of thinking?

2. Biblical witness

A spiritual appreciation of the child pervades the whole Judaeo-Christian tradition. Given the extent of the data, we confine ourselves here to some few points. For instance, Jesus' teaching must be located in his own Jewish world and its rejection of the violence of the Gentile world against children, as with child-sacrifice, exposure and abortion amongst others.[9] Furthermore, in that Jewish tradition, 'The surprising, apparently arbitrary primacy of the youngest child'[10] is a constant theme in the sacred writings of Israel, as in the case of Abel, Isaac, Jacob, Joseph, Ephraim, David and Solomon. It points to a divine reversal of values, and God's absolute freedom, as Paul came to experience: 'My grace is sufficient for

---

7. It would be intriguing to relate this phenomenological approach with Philip L Reynolds's informative study, 'Thomas Aquinas and the Paradigms of Childhood', in Brennan, *The Vocation of the Child*, but that would take another essay.

8. For a profound meditation on these points, see Karl Rahner, 'Ideas for a Theology of Childhood', in *Theological Investigations VIII*, translated by David Bourke (New York: Herder and Herder, 1971), 33–50; also, Christoph Potworowski, 'The Attitude of the Child in the Theology of Han Urs von Balthasar', in *Communio* 22 (Spring 1995): 44–55.

9. See Charles J Reid, 'The Rights of Children in Medieval Canon Law', in Brennan *The Vocation of the Child* for valuable references.

10. Robin Maas, 'Christ as the Logos of Childhood: Reflections on the Meaning and Mission of the Child', in *Theology Today* (1999): 459.

you, for my power is made perfect in weakness' (2 Cor 12:9). The divine favour rests to a surprising degree on those who are most vulnerable, 'the little ones', that are invisible in the harsh demands of social life.

Note, too, that the 'lost' or 'inner child' of modern pop-psychology is never the issue. Rather, the challenge resides in the vocation that is common to all. It consists in allowing oneself to be born anew into the realm of eternal life. Such life is the gift of One who is the source of life. All are called to union with and in Christ. He is at once the eternal Son of the Father, and 'the first-born of all creation' (Col 1:16). The important point in this perspective is that becoming like a child is the goal, not just a stage that is to be left behind.

The gospel's account of the Child Jesus being brought to the temple communicates both a sense of promise and crisis: he will be a sign of contradiction and judgment (Lk 2:34–8). Pharoah's mass infanticide was perpetrated in order to control the Jewish slave population in Egypt, yet it led to the deliverance of the Exodus. Likewise, Herod's slaughter of the innocents promised something new.[11]

The novelty of what Jesus promises can be described from a number of converging perspectives.[12] Children are at once the recipients, models and the measure of the Kingdom of God. They are its special recipients (see Mk 10:13–16// Mt 19:13–15; Lk 18:15–17). Jesus blesses little children brought to him and teaches that the reign of God belongs to them. Children evoke the spirit of the beatitudes (Mt 5:3–12; Lk 6:20–23)—in contrast to the egocentric self-assertiveness of adults. Because children are not full of themselves, they anticipate the character of the Kingdom as a 'kingdom of nobodies', the poor and the powerless who are most receptive to the gift of God: 'Whoever

11. Maas, 'Christ as the Logos of Childhood', 460.
12. See Judith Gundry-Volf, '"To such as these belong the Reign of God": Jesus and Children", in *Theology Today* (1999): 469–80.

does not receive the reign of God as a child will not enter it (Mk 10:15). Such a statement was subversive to Jewish—and Hellenistic—sensibilities. It suggested that the much-prized attainments of wisdom and fidelity to the law were being demeaned. What mattered most was to receive everything as a pure gift. And so the challenge: 'unless you change and become like children, you will never enter the kingdom of heaven' (Mt 18:1–5). It is children who recognise Christ, and, in their humble receptivity, come to know what has been revealed (Mt 21:14–16// Lk 10:21).[13]

Children, and 'little ones' generally, are the object of God's special care: 'so it is not the will of your Father in heaven that one of these little ones be lost' (Mt 18:10–14). The role of authority is not self-promotion, but realised in service of those who are powerless: 'Whoever welcomes one such child in my name, welcomes me, and whoever welcomes me welcomes not me but the one who sent me' (Mk 9:33–7 and parallels). In her dependence, trust and powerlessness, the child has been described as the *real presence* of Christ—a living sacrament of the kingdom of heaven'.[14] The vulnerability of Jesus himself is evoked ('in my name'), as well as his origin in the one who sent him—the generative mystery of the Father. In short, the reign of God is a world of children, children of the Father, children united in the Son and breathing his Spirit, living from him who is the first born from the dead.

This is a brief indication of the field of meaning in which the child is presented in the New Testament. Spirituality, Christian or otherwise, cannot ignore what the Scriptures suggest. It leaves all of us to wonder whether we have been rather too 'adult' in our understanding of the ways of God and the living out of our different vocations.

---

13. For further reference, see Elmer J Thiessen, 'The Vocation of the Child as Learner', in Brennan, *The Vocation of the Child*.
14. Maas, 'Christ as the Logos of Childhood', 458.

3. Conclusion

Friedrich Nietzsche anticipated a stage in culture when self-vaunting freedom would be the fundamental value of the 'New Man'. Yet, as a stage in this self-realisation, the great soul needs to undergo three metamorphoses—from camel to lion, and then, from lion to child.[15] The camel, staggering under the responsibilities of a new freedom, wanders into the desert. There, a metamorphosis occurs: by disencumbering its freedom from its moral burdens, the camel becomes a lion, the lord of the desert, asserting its power and will over all else. But, before that wilful domination can occur, it must become a child, in 'innocence, forgetfulness, a new beginning—a sacred Yes to the new world in which it is born'.[16] The burdens of the past—above all the Judaeo-Christian past—must be cast into oblivion, so that an untrammelled, wide-eyed innocence in a new phase of history can begin.

Over a century after Nietzsche wrote those words, we are aware of the miseries resulting from the growth of 'the child' that he envisaged. The egomanic assertive freedom that Nietzsche encouraged failed to bring about a new world. As a result, serious thinkers become more 'camel-like' than ever. They live in a certain depression, wandering in a cultural desert. They become overloaded with responsibilities in their awareness of the dwindling of hope for the new and the more humane. And yet, in this dispirited, overloaded phase of spirituality, the phenomenon of the child refreshes spirituality at its roots. In a world of violent competition and the exponential growth of problems and responsibilities, the child calls for the rebirth of wonder, trust and playful contentment

---

15. See Friedrich Nietzsche, *Thus Spoke Zarathustra: A Book for Everyone*, translation and introduction by RJ Hollingdale (London: Penguin), 54–5.
16. Nietzsche, *Thus Spoke Zarathustra*, 55.

within the great womb of life and time. The harried adult might see only problems, and become weary in mind and heart. Children live otherwise. They breathe another air, content to play within the inexhaustible mystery of what has been so uncannily given. Every child is a call to return to the gift that was at the beginning, is now, and ever shall be.

Children, Church and the Problem of Boredom

Joyce A Mercer
Virginia, USA

On a given Sunday morning in homes across the United States, and perhaps other First World contexts as well,[1] among the many conversations taking place between children and their parents/caregivers are several concerning the problem of boredom. Children protest their parents' efforts to get them ready for church with words such as, 'But I don't want to go to Sunday School. It's too boring'. Parents, worried about instilling negative associations into their children concerning church, fear taking children into a full worship service out of concern that the children may be bored. 'I'd rather wait until she's old enough to understand what is happening before I have her in the service. I don't want her to be bored, and start thinking of church as boring', one mother put it. Children, youth, and adults alike evaluate their experiences of worship, Christian Education, fellowship, and mission engagement in the church on the basis of the ability of these experiences of

---

1. I write specifically in relation to the context I know best, namely North America and the US. I believe, however, that many of the same dynamics of consumerism and the construction of children as consumers take place in other contexts (particularly those of similar affluence). In addition, I am aware that not all children or even all North American children are positioned in the same way in relation to late capitalism's consumerist practices. Some children relate to the economy as producers, and may be excluded by poverty from participation in the full range of consumer practices I describe here.

church life to hold their interest and command their attention, or, put differently, to escape being boring.

This essay explores the problem of boredom as a key aspect of consumer culture affecting the religious and spiritual lives of children today. The market's influential reshaping of childhood as a time of ceaseless desire for novelty, and of children themselves as persons developmentally in need of continual stimulation, supports the production and sale of consumer goods designed to address such 'needs' in children. In the process, however, parenting, education, and other practices of care for children also take on new shapes, organised around the necessity of preventing or dispelling children's boredom. I argue that contemporary expectations that children's external environments and relationships must protect them from boredom derive from consumer culture's influence on childhood rather than from the inherent needs of children. Such expectations therefore must be questioned and critiqued in relation to non-market derived criteria supportive of the spiritual well-being and thriving of children.

1. Expecting to be bored

No one likes to be bored, and yet most people probably can recall being bored from time to time. A long wait to see a doctor, an uninteresting lecture or sermon, or a cross-country flight are opportunities for boredom that many people experience at some time. While some overly active persons may long for a temporary respite from activity and stimulation, such times apart differ from the state known as boredom. (In fact, we call the former times 'vacation'.) Boredom is the situation in which any sense of interest, excitement, or drive is absent, an unwelcome and uncomfortable state in which there is no activation of desire in a person. Boredom may be occasioned by an absence of stimulation, as often happens, for example, with a long car trip across a flat, unchanging countryside with no companion or radio to provide contrast to the emptiness of the activity and its setting. Or, in the opposite extreme, boredom may also be occasioned by the presence of an excess of stimulation, such that nothing stands out and one's interest and attention fail to be activated by anything in particular. This latter type of boredom comes into focus in caricatures of affluent children surrounded by toys, who nevertheless look to their parents complaining, 'I'm bored—there's nothing to do here'.

Social historians identify the problem of boredom as a relatively recent phenomenon, particularly in its expected occurrence among children. Prior to World War II there was little mention of boredom in relation to children. In fact, the main concern with boredom found expression in etiquette-and advice-literature about how to avoid *being boring*.[2] After World War II, being bored took on greater significance than being boring. Before that time, boredom was more of a condition of existence than a feeling. From the late 1940's on, it was 'an inflicted state demanding correction by others'.[3]

Close parallels to the phenomenon of boredom certainly existed in earlier times, in forms such as the medieval concept of *acedia* (also known as 'sloth' and named as one of the 'seven deadly sins', a state of spiritual dullness and disinterest), or the later Renaissance concept of *melancholia* (a persistent and oppressive form of sorrow or depression). As Patricia Meyer Spacks[4] notes, however, the idea of boredom as it is used today to connote an 'all embracing explanation for psychic distress' is rather new. These days, boredom functions as the '*diagnosis de*

2.   PN Stearns, *Anxious Parents: A History of Modern Childrearing in America* (New York: New York University Press, 2003), 17.
3.   *Ibid*, 196.
4.   PAM Spacks, *Boredom: The Literary History of a State of Mind* (Chicago: University of Chicago Press, 1995), 4.

jour', attributed to pre-verbal three month old babies by their parents as an explanation for fussiness, as well as being offered as the explanation for why teenagers use drugs and commit crimes.[5] As an 'embracing rubric of discontent',[6] boredom thus has come to be viewed as both a normal and expected state yet one so uncomfortable that persons will go to great lengths to prevent or alleviate it. Boredom's rise coincides with (Western) modernity's and postmodernity's greater emphasis upon autonomy, subjectivity and individualism.[7]

When children today complain of being bored, the state of which they speak differs considerably from its earlier cousins acedia and melancholy in terms of causality. These historically earlier cousins of boredom referenced a condition interpreted as the responsibility of the bearer. For example, a monk suffering from acedia was not the victim of dull surroundings but was a person committing a sin—the sin of disinterest and detachment from the love of spiritual practices. Melancholy, similarly, referred to a state of discontent originating from within the person bearing it.

By contrast to both of these conditions, contemporary notions of boredom locate its causes outside of the person. Boredom happens because of an environment that fails to be sufficiently interesting. It is the result of an *external* lack or failure, rather than an internal problem for which the bearer holds responsibility. In this contemporary view, boredom is an externally caused state to which one falls victim. When a child complains of being bored, she registers a complaint that a problem exists 'out there' that ought to be righted by someone else (such as a parent or teacher). Implicit expectations that external environments must provide something stimulating, and that parents and other caregivers hold responsibility for

---

5.   *Ibid*, 251.
6.   *Ibid*, x.
7.   *Ibid*, x.

preventing and alleviating children's boredom, seldom come under scrutiny. The co-occurrence of childhood and boredom has become normalised, as has the concomitant coupling of the work of parenting and the squelching of opportunities for children to become bored.

2. Consumer culture and bored children

How did boredom become such an expected feature of childhood, and one for which parents bear so much responsibility? The answers to this question lie in the convergence between certain postmodern cultural forms shaping constructions of childhood, and the rise of consumerism as a way of life under late globalised capitalism. When scholars of contemporary culture depict the features that define postmodernity, they describe the emergence of certain cultural elements such as the tendency toward erasure of boundaries between art, entertainment, and advertising; a continual quest for novelty; the importance of image and the visual; the compression of time and space by technology such as the internet; and an emphasis on intense experiences and 'spectacle'.

So, for example, in postmodern North America, when a child sits down to breakfast, that child may pour cereal from a box that proclaims in words and images that this breakfast will be an event. It will be a fun, exciting experience (not to be confused with the mere address of the body's nutritional needs). The pictured characters on the box, well known to children from their promulgation through television, internet, and billboard advertising, also appear as characters in children's cartoons and films, and may be sold as toy 'action figures' for play. In this example, the ordinary activity of eating breakfast becomes a kind of spectacle, transformed from mere eating to an event replete with expectations of novelty and fun in which the boundaries between the entertainment provided by cartoon characters and their functions as marketing figures have become nonexistent. Merely eating breakfast would be boring by comparison.

Such features, described above as cultural forms of postmodernity, occur in conjunction with the elevation of consumerism as an economic structure and cultural form in affluent societies such as North America today. Consumerism refers to the situation in which a society structures its life around practices of consumption. Consumption, of course, is not limited to the discrete moment of purchasing of goods, but encompasses the whole range of actions oriented toward procuring, using, and eventually disposing of a consumable good. In this understanding, time spent looking at advertising, thinking about a purchase, and planning for it comprise consumer practices, as do the actual purchase and use of a product.[8]

In a consumerist society even the most fundamental elements of social life, such as the establishment and maintenance of social bonds between people or the means by which persons define and demonstrate their identities to one another, take place through consumption. For example, two young people may meet for the first time on the basketball park of an urban park. Both wear the same brand of athletic shoes and can make reference to advertising images related to sports that provide a level of instantaneous connection. Perhaps these same young people also communicate something about their age and class identity by wearing other clothing marked with product logos or words. 'Gap' written across the front of the

---

8.   JA Mercer, *Welcoming Children: A Practical Theology of Childhood* (St Louis, Missouri: Chalice, 2005) and VJ Miller, *Consuming Religion: Christian Faith and Practice in a Consumer Culture* (New York and London: Continuum, 2004).

sweatshirt proclaims a different group identity that does the shirt that says 'Abercrombie and Fitch'. In these examples, the practices of consumption through which persons acquire particular brands of clothing facilitate social connections and communicate identity in contemporary postmodern contexts where more traditional markers of connection and identity (for example kinship networks, neighborhood affiliations) may no longer operate.

I explore in considerable detail elsewhere processes of economic transition in relation to the development of North American consumer culture, from its roots in early capitalism to Keynesian-Fordist capitalism of the mid-twentieth century and then to what is often referred to as late globalised capitalism of the present time.[9] While I cannot fully address that process in the space of this essay, it is important to note the developing coherence between the needs and values of the marketplace today and contemporary constructions of children as *consumers par excellence*. In postmodernity, cultural and economic forces participate in constructing a consuming child whose very existence as a child has come to be defined in terms of an appetite for continually new and stimulating experiences, satisfied by consumer products. Lacking such stimulation, children become bored. In effect, consumer culture constructs 'the bored child' as the antithesis, and necessary support for, its larger construction of 'the child as consumer'.

---

9. D Harvey, *The Condition of Postmodernity: An Enquiry Into the Origins of Cultural Change* (Cambridge, Massachusetts: Blackwell, 1990), see also JA Mercer, *Welcoming Children, op cit*, and J Miller, *Consuming Religion, op cit*.

3. Combating boredom with consumption: The spiritual malaise of excess

In an economy over-saturated with goods, the market needs children to be consumers of the goods it produces and sells. Consumer children are targets of advertising with real buying power. Susan Linn, co-founder of the Coalition for a Commercial Free Childhood, notes that in the US advertisers now spend around $16 billion US dollars per year advertising to children. Children, for their part, influence the spending of some $600 billion US dollars annually.[10] Obviously there is a limit to the amount of consumer goods persons purchase sheerly out of need. So in order to maintain the level of mass consumption that will support increasing production of goods in a contemporary consumer-driven economy, new markets must be found or created, and new appetites for goods must be stimulated. A look at advertising over the last fifty years shows the emergence of children as just such a new market for consumable goods, and of advertising to and through children as a means to stimulate continuing consumption in a product-saturated environment.

Sociologist Daniel Cook[11] details the relationship between the development of increasingly narrow age-segmented groupings for children in the US during the twentieth century, and the appearance of products such as toddler toys and furniture. Such products come to be associated with good nurturing parenting in which parents seek the growth of their children, facilitated by the use of age-specific products marketed as specially designed (and necessary) for this age

---

10.   At <http://www.susanlinn.net/facts_about_marketing.htm>. Accessed 4 February 2007.

11.   DT Cook, 'The Rise of "The Toddler" as Subject and as Merchandising Category in the 1930s', in *New Forms of Consumption: Consumers, Culture, and Commodification*, edited by M Gottdiener (Boulder, Colorado and New York: Rowman and Littlefield, 2000).

group. At the same time, by decreasing the span of months or years in these age groups for which products are designed, marketers insure continued consumption of goods by parents concerned to have the 'right' products for their child's development who must buy new products when their children move into a new age cohort.

This market-driven, age-based segmenting of childhood into increasingly small increments finds a worthy parallel in those cultural forms associated with postmodernity examined above, that emphasise fragmented attention, ceaseless quests for novel experiences, and the centrality of *spectacle* for everyday life. I along with Sharon Stephens[12] have argued that such a coherence between cultural forms of postmodernity and the economic forces of late globalised capitalism, in fact reshapes what childhood is and what it means to be a child today. Such reshaping of contemporary constructions of childhood matters not only at the level of ideas about children, but also in the real experiences and material conditions of children's lives today. Children now 'need' goods that did not even exist in the recent past. Their continuing development and growth supposedly hinges upon access to a wide variety of goods, from age-graded and gender-distinctive disposable diapers to the small sized toddler bed that replaces the crib—only to be replaced shortly by a standard sized bed in child-themed decorations that will be outgrown at puberty necessitating yet another purchase. The success of the market in co-opting the growth-language and agenda of early childhood education, reshaped in terms of how consumption aids parents in their task by insuring the growth of children, is close to astounding.

Defining children rather exclusively in terms of a discourse of growth defines parents as people whose primary work is the

---

12. S Stephens, 'Children and the Politics of Culture in Late Capitalism', in *Children and the Politics of Culture*, edited by S Stephens (Princeton, New Jersey: Princeton University Press, 1995), 3–48.

facilitation of that growth. That is not a particularly unexpected understanding of parenting *per se*. What is problematic, however, is consumer culture's reification of growth as the solely relevant aspect of childhood, and its effective defining of parental efforts to facilitate children's growth in terms of the purchase of consumer goods. Marketers have effectively harnessed the growth-oriented discourse of contemporary understandings of childhood and parenting, producing a range of consumer goods claiming to assist in facilitating children's growth. Good parenting comes to mean buying the things (or purchasing the experiences) that enhance children's growth.

The parallel to this construction of parenting in contemporary constructions of childhood is the idea that children by nature require continual stimulation. The market economy thus produces childhood as a time defined by the constant quest for novelty and 'fun'. Failure to provide it risks the possibility of arresting growth. In the absence of entertainment, distraction, or some other kind of stimulation, children might become bored. Because of this link between constant stimulation and growth, boredom easily comes to be seen as the enemy of children's thriving and a sign of inadequate parenting. As social historian Peter N Sterns notes, consumerism 'pushed parents to redefine their own obligations to children and to assume responsibility for children's fun . . . Ultimately, new commitments to entertain children would become commitments to banish boredom.'[13]

After World War II, Sterns continues, the parental responsibility to prevent children's boredom became a major feature in increased parental anxiety in the US: '. . . boredom began to shift to children, which meant . . . that responsibility for avoiding or pulling children out of boredom became a significant parental charge. The bored child became something else for parents to worry about, and the fault lay outside the

---

13. Stearns, *Anxious Parents, op cit*, 169.

child himself.'[14] Anxious parents and bored children prove a profitable combination for the entertainment industry and toy markets.

I do not intend here to reduce children or parents to these constructions of boredom and anxiety without remainder. Clearly, children and parents in their actual lives are far more complex than this. I place so much stress upon the power of market capitalism to shape notions of childhood and parenting, however, for a very simple reason: these social constructions of children and their caregivers have very real effects on the actual, everyday lives of children and parents. In the concluding section of this essay, then, I turn to address how the close relationship between boredom and childhood that has become part of the definition of childhood since the late 1940's relates to children's religious lives.

4. Bored children, anxious parents, and faith communities

The children and parents making their way through the doors of church sanctuaries and Christian Education halls on Sunday mornings are the same 'bored children' and 'anxious adults' who multitask their way through a myriad of consumer choices throughout the week. What do these constructions mean for the religious lives of children and, by extension, of those adults most deeply involved in their care? While many implications present themselves, two stand out as particularly significant.

First, the spiritual problem of children's boredom goes beyond a temporary negative feeling, to the more fundamental issue of a child's capacities *to attend* to things that matter outside of the self and understand them as meaningful. As noted earlier, boredom may result from a lack of expected stimulation in a child's environment (and environments constantly populated with media and other forms of entertainment

---

14.   Stearns, *Anxious Parents, op cit*, 171.

create considerably heightened expectations). Boredom dulls the imagination's ability to attribute positive significance to such a situation, which may be incorrectly interpreted from the point of view of deficit or lack.

But a child may also be bored when surrounded by stimuli, even in excess. Regular experiences of such boredom may well produce children who become unable to determine what is significant and what is not significant in their environments, such that their desire cannot attach to anything in particular. When there is so much stimulation that it comes to be expected, children and adults alike may fall into what Michael Reposa[15] understands boredom to be about: 'the lack of a capacity to discern the full significance of a thing or a situation'—in other words, the inability to understand something as meaningful.

Children's spirituality entails a continual activity of 'meaning making'—of rendering experiences, symbols, stories, and relationships meaningful in particular ways. Just today, an Episcopal priest spoke to me about a child in her parish who, upon hearing the Palm Sunday story and liturgy last week, commented that even 'dumb and stubborn' creatures must matter to Jesus, as he began and ended his life on donkeys. This child used her recollection of other stories about Jesus in combination with experiences/knowledge of donkeys and the Palm Sunday story of Jesus riding into Jerusalem on a donkey, to construct a new understanding about Jesus' care for all kinds of creatures.

Children at all levels of cognitive, physical, and emotional development, constantly interpret the world around them, including the world of their faith community and its sacred stories. They may do so in nonverbal ways, such as a baby smiling back at the affirmation mirrored in the long, loving look

---

15. ML Raposa, *Boredom and the Religious Imagination* (Charlottesville: University Press of Virginia, 1999), 14.

of a mother or father, or a child's drawing of images from the scripture passages read in the morning liturgy. 'Discerning the full significance of a thing' does not have to look the same for children as it might for adults. Children's spirituality involves attending and discerning according to their own capacities as children. It entails meaning-making in the ways that fit children's consciousness.

In order to engage in such meaning-making activity in any form, however, children must be able to attribute significance to what they hear, see, feel, and encounter. Boredom attacks and disables a child's ability to recognise significance, because in boredom nothing seems worthy of the attachment of one's interest, attention and desire. In an over saturated, excessively stimulating environment, no single object, relationship, or situation is selected out for attention by a bored child, amidst all the competing possibilities. In the context where stimulation is absent, as might be the case, for instance, in a service of worship or prayer practice utilising silence, a bored child accustomed to constant novelty becomes unable to attach positive significance to silence and stillness.

A second, powerful effect on children's spirituality from the market-driven ideology of boredom as an inevitable feature of childhood is its self-referential bent. The widespread embrace of children's boredom as an explanation for various problematic behaviors, together with parental anxieties about preventing and alleviating children's boredom, leads to the constant evaluation of religious experience in terms of its 'entertainment value'. One pastor friend of mine remarked recently that at least during the liturgical season of Lent, when he tended to focus his sermons on various difficult experiences of pathos in human life, he wished that people would stop coming out of church to greet him by saying, 'I enjoyed your sermon, Pastor'. Anxious parents ask children if they 'had fun' in Sunday school, and decide what congregational activities to participate in based upon whether these activities include sufficient entertainment for children. In other words, when children's participation in faith communities revolves around the prevention or alleviation of boredom, the experience of church becomes self-referentially about the child and her or his feeling state.

A central claim of the Christian faith is that because God is *pro nobis* (for us) in Christ, in the church we therefore are constituted as a people 'for others'. For Christians, then, the primary rationale for participation in any church activity is that doing so directs our attention to God, and equips us to participate with God in God's activities of love, justice, and reconciliation in the world. We are Christians not for ourselves but as the Body of Christ poured out for the life of the world.

Churches have not always been very skilled at involving children in practices of service, ministry, and care for others. Church life tends to situate children as the objects of its educational efforts, rather than as child-practitioners of a living faith. However, children's spirituality is by its constitution a relational experience,[16] in which the human capacities for empathy and compassion that develop fairly early in life come into play in the ways children attempt to care with and for others. For example, children often identify with those who are smaller, less powerful, and weaker. Stories of hurt people or animals prompt outpourings of empathic regard from children, who find various ways to act in compassion for others.

Boredom and its self-referential focus can easily disable empathy and compassion for others with its requirement that a child's and parent's live revolve around its banishment. Church becomes another form of entertainment rather than a place to seek encounter with God and Christian community. Boredom impairs the ability to act because 'the sufferer from boredom

---

16. D Hay and R Nye, *The Spirit of the Child* (London: HarperCollins, 1998).

finds it impossible to invest fully in any action, to relieve any action with the effort of involvement'.[17] Bored children are impaired in their capacities to act on behalf of others. That is a spiritual problem of considerable consequence in a world crying for persons who can act in compassion, care, and empathy.

Third, because children like adults live out their spirituality in relation to their missteps, faults, and mistakes and not only in acts of goodness, generosity and kindness, children's spiritualities include practices for dealing with these 'unlovely' aspects of their lives. I know a child who has a very short temper. Inclined toward name calling and even swearing when seized by his anger, he almost always immediately regrets doing so because he is aware of the power of words and the hurt they can cause. I have seen him seek to amends with persons he called some horrible name only moments earlier, willing to acknowledge the wrong he has done and seek restoration of the relationship even at cost of some shame or self-humbling. Sometimes his efforts are rejected. Yet he continues to risk this rejection, as he also works toward having more control of his emotions and stopping the problematic behavior. What I am describing here is a child's spirituality that includes the hopeful possibility that one can live through mistakes and try again.

Boredom covers human failings in apathy and indifference, a situation in which persons neither care enough to forgive or not to forgive. Bored children may not be sufficiently aware of their own inner lives (even at whatever is a developmentally appropriate level for a particular child) or of the impact of their words and actions on the lives of others to seek reconciliation. Boredom's supposed inevitability in children, then, circumvents the relational spiritual practices of reconciliation

---

17. Spacks, *Boredom: The Literary History of a State of Mind, op cit*, 251.

and redress of wrongdoing of which children are capable and in need.

5. Rejecting the possibility of boredom

Is boredom ever 'real'? I have been talking about boredom as a social construction, which can sound as if it is made up or imaginary. Certainly there are circumstances having little to do with the influences of consumer culture, in which there actually is nothing of interest, no object or situation to which significance may be attached. There are, for instance, circumstances of temporary stasis in which otherwise alert and attentive persons become bored by virtue of the genuine inability to find anything meaningful in the situation. Waiting in a long queue comes to mind as an example.

There also are tedious, repetitive forms of labor that evoke genuine boredom in forms that fall outside the social constructions I have discussed above. I do not mean to trivialise such situations in my discussion of the construction of children's boredom as a spiritual problem. The role of consumer market culture in creating such situations and their differential occurrence among non-dominant groups such as people who are poor, would be another worthy exploration but lies beyond the scope of my endeavor. To bring the matter back to children, their construction by consumer culture does not rule out the significance of their experiences as bored people. It does, however, call on persons who care about the thriving of children and their spirituality to 'problematise' the tight relationship between bored children, anxious parents, and market place profits.

One strategy for countering the pervasive power of this reshaping of childhood in relation to boredom is to reject it as an appropriate, necessary way to define childhood. In my fifth grade year, I had a teacher in school who responded to children's claims of boredom in two ways. If time were an issue, she would simply lob a well-worn aphorism at the child: 'Boredom doesn't exist, only boring people. See if you can figure out what your problem is and do something about it.' If she had time, though, she likely would engage in a longer conversation, saying something like, 'Well, let's see about that. What interesting things are you missing right now? What is not happening in your imagination?' I cannot recall a single instance in which the conversation that unfolded from there ended in a child's claim of continuing boredom. Basically my teacher, Miss Marguerite Pease, rejected the possibility of children defining themselves in terms of boredom.

What if faith communities and the adults most closely related to children within them similarly rejected boredom as a defining feature of childhood? What if these adults regularly invited children to participate with them in the undulating rhythms of practices of stillness and silence (for example, contemplation, quiet prayer or reflection) and those of action and movement (active service, joyful praise, movement), reinterpreting the former as opportunities to encounter the holy rather than as contexts entrapping persons in boredom?

In cultures centered upon consumption, marketers hope that adults will not notice how 'unnatural' is the notion of boredom's inevitability in childhood. Treating the association between boredom and childhood as 'natural' and normal, the market generously offers to solve this problem for parents and other caregivers anxious to avert this experience in children's lives. The temptation I observe in myself as a parent and among other adult caregivers is to meet the claim of children's boredom with lists of 'things to do' that will relieve it. A more helpful strategy would be to help children develop an alternative vocabulary for naming the experiences they (and we) currently classify as boredom. What feelings are at work? What else is operating under this catch-all rubric that children can learn to describe and address with different language?

Christian spirituality offers some help in this regard, with its broad nomenclature for human experience ranging from restlessness, tiredness, emptiness, awe, grief, fear, and jubilation, to thirst, penitence, contentment, confusion, and anxiety.

Someone once said that the ability to name one's self and one's experience belongs to the powerful. Perhaps among most significant actions of child empowerment engaged in by adult companions of children today are those that help children name themselves and their experiences. The ability to name childhood not in the distorted language of market culture, but in the rich tones of faith traditions that honor children, is both a strategy of resisting the power of market culture over children's live, and of supporting the strong, relational, and compassionate spiritual lives of children.

Media Narratives as a Concept for Spiritual Development

C Glenn Cupit
Adelaide

The importance of narrative in spirituality is largely uncontested. Historically, people structured their world understanding through stories of gods, demigods and heroes. The Bible is neither theological tome, nor moral treatise, nor historical record, though it incorporates elements of each. Rather it is essentially a collection of narratives from which those elements are derived. Non-religious traditions also have stories which express their spiritual substance, whether 'scientific' ('big bang' cosmology, evolution), or 'folk-wisdom', (ancestral healers, 'cautionary tales'). We accord cultural importance to all 'tellers of tales'. Their narratives transmit the spiritual culture of communities to successive generations.

With the rise to importance of narratives transmitted via electronic media it becomes important to consider how the specific characteristics of those media and of children's spirituality intersect to identify the impact of such narratives as the context within which children's spirituality develops.

1. Children's exposure to media narratives

Traditionally, spiritually relevant stories were transmitted orally through parents, priests, teachers, and other recognised raconteurs, though manuscripts served an educated few. Only culturally approved narratives were transmitted to children, except perhaps for illicit tales of disreputable old men (and perhaps women). Where literacy became common, particularly with the development of printing, text became influential, though its impact was tempered by parents, schools and the state limiting children's access. But print makes subversive narratives potentially available, as evidenced by Protestant printing of vernacular Bibles and Galileo's writings.

The twentieth century saw the emergence and progressive proliferation of audio-visual narratives, initially through film where, to some extent, parental control and government censorship limited exposure. Availability accelerated with the advent of electronic media, first television, then video, and more recently computers and the world wide web, largely supplanting print media.[1] Despite the best efforts of advocacy groups, legislators and censors, this has been a Pandora's box as no effort suffices to control children's access to an incredible variety of narratives, many deemed inappropriate by parents, educators and clergy. It is important to understand the impact of this new genre of narratives on children's spirituality.

2. The baggage of spirituality

No approach to spirituality is independent of the presuppositions of the writer, and there is a wide range of ideologies in recent writing. I have identified three distinct ideological clusters within this literature: 'naturalistic', spirituality as a part of the mundane world, usually the best or 'highest' aspects of the person; 'romantic', connectedness to an impersonal cosmic 'consciousness', 'force' or 'principle', usually represented as benevolent; and 'theistic', relationship to (a) self-aware transcendent entity(-ies), usually a god or gods.[2]

1.   David Carr, 'Moral Education at the Movies: On the Cinematic Treatment of Morally Significant Story and Narrative', *Journal of Moral Education*, 35/3 (2006): 319–33.

2.   C Glenn Cupit, *A Critical Evaluation of Biblical Perspectives on Spiritual Development and of Dynamic Systems Theory to Identify Major Implications for Public Educative Care of Children* (Doctoral

Undisclosed ideological underpinnings foster confusion and militate against effective dialogue. Even basic definitions can *a priori* exclude certain understandings. For instance, the very inclusive definition provided to guide these contributions[3] still excludes the many approaches which lack a transcendental element. My stance is based on a critical evangelical hermeneutic using their overall biblical treatment both to define both spirituality and childhood, and to identify the nature of childhood spirituality. The understanding of development is based on dynamic systems theory.[4] I argue this in full elsewhere;[5] here there is only room to assert the conclusions.

Though the Bible does not use the term, 'spirituality' is represented as a consequence of encounters with entities metaphorically akin to the wind or breath. These 'spirits' are morally bipolar; good identified with God's action in the world, evil with any influence antagonistic to the divine benevolence. Humans are spirits instantiated in flesh. Other spirits are also instantiated in aspects of the material world; groups, institutions, belief systems, communities, perhaps even idols. But each spirit transcends the limits of corporeality. With the

---

dissertation, Murdoch University, Perth, Murdoch University Digital Theses, URL: <http://wwwlib.murdoch.edu.au/adt/browse/view/adt-MU20051129.114720>, 2002), 60–82.

3. Maria Harris and Gabriel Moran, *Reshaping Religious Education* (Louisville: Westminster John Knox, 1998).

4. For example, Mark Howe and Marc Lewis, 'The Importance of Dynamic Systems Approaches for Understanding Development', *Developmental Review*, 25, (2005): 247–51. See also Esther Thelen and Linda Smith, 'Dynamic Systems Theories', in *Handbook of Child Psychology*, edited by William Damon and Richard Lerner (New York: Wiley, 1998).

5. Cupit, *A Critical Evaluation of Biblical Perspectives on Spiritual Development, op cit*, 257–317, and C Glenn Cupit, *Perspectives on Children and Spirituality* (Central Coast: Scripture Union Australia, 2005), 99–138.

exception of God's Spirit, far from being eternal, spirits are created and, lacking a determination by God, dissipate with the phenomena which are their instantiation. Humans, as spirits, encounter and interact with other spirits, usually mediated through everyday experiences. Adults are called to commit their spirits to the Spirit of God. Otherwise they submit, actively or passively, to spiritual evil; equivocation is not possible. Such a demand is not applied to children, as addressed below.

3. The limits of childhood

Alexander asserts: 'Childhood, as we understand it today, is a product of post-Enlightenment romanticism . . . The Bible, therefore, contains no clearly defined picture of the child'.[6] That biblical authors had a different concept of childhood does not mean they had no concept. Their picture of the child is well drawn, if unromantic.

Biblical childhood was functional rather than chronological. The only 'age' which might serve as a *terminus ad quem* in the Old Testament is twenty, when men became subject to the census and draft, but it is doubtful that this related to a perceived end of childhood. Similarly, the New Testament makes no theological point of age despite Crompton's claim that childhood's end was the onset of puberty, signalled by the eruption of a second pubic hair.[7] 'Childhood' was defined by dependence on the direction and nurture of others. The terms for child (all eleven of them) indicate a characteristic (like 'toddler') or limitation (as 'pre-pubescent'). 'Children' lacked moral discernment, ability to understand, practical sense,

---

6.   HA Alexander, 'A Jewish View of Human Learning', *International Journal of Children's Spirituality* 4/2 (1999): 155.

7.   Margaret Crompton, *Children, Spirituality, Religion and Social Work* (Ashgate: Aldershot, 1998).

ability to express themselves, and power. They could also be those who, though not young, share such characteristics either involuntarily, as the retarded, the possessed, and even the helplessly ill; or voluntarily, as disciples were urged.

What harmonises such depictions is that children lacked the competency, position or power to decide and act as they wish on their own behalf. They were necessarily under the care and authority of adults, especially their parents, with whom they were identified and shared common fate, except where God directly intervened on their behalf as 'father of orphans'.

In the biblical text, a child is a person (of any age), who is unable, for any reason, to exercise autonomous competence but relies on others to take care of, and decide for, them.

4. The peculiarity of children's spirituality

Much of the expressed concern about media centres on the effect its narratives have on children, with violence, sexuality and bad language dominating the discourse, though recently advertising unhealthy food has emerged.[8] This assumes children are particularly vulnerable to such narratives.

Setting aside the occasional hysteria of such concerns, children are different from adults in the way they relate to their world and consequently acutely susceptible. This reflects the distinctive nature of their spirituality. This peculiarity has been a matter of considerable debate, especially within evangelical Christianity, with conflict centred on Jesus' assertion that the kingdom of heaven belongs 'to such', and on what characteristics of children led Jesus to this claim. Buckland refutes the common identification of various subjective qualities because they are not true of all children.[9] He suggests an

8.   Judith Van Evra, *Television and Child Development*, third edition (Hillsdale: Lawrence Erlbaum Associates, 2004).

9.   Ron Buckland, *Children and the King* (Melbourne: ANZEA, 1977) and *Children and God* (Homebush West: ANZEA, 1988).

'objective' quality, children's 'helplessness' to determine their own spiritual state. This advances our understanding but requires a further shift to adequately reflect the complexity of spiritual encounter and the developmental nature of children.

No single term accurately represents children's spiritual life but a metaphor of 'relative openness' has much to recommend it. This depicts children as born like an unprotected community, with no spiritual defences at all and entirely accessible to any spiritual influence they encounter (so 'helpless' also resonates). This is openness both to good and to evil, and as much to mediate as to direct spiritual influence. As they grow and experience life, children become increasingly able to defend themselves and to rebuff spiritual influence, but this is contingent on the influences' strength and persistence. The older they are, the stronger the narrative has to be in order to break through their defences. A person ceases to be a child only when, like a walled and armed city, they are able to resist spiritual influence, and persist in that resistance over time, even when unsupported by others.

5. Electronic narratives and spiritual agency

Electronic narratives are a fusion of artefact and word; of artistry and truth, or ugliness and error. They carry significant spiritual force as they interact with the spirits of the audience, for good or ill, because human and other spirits are present in works of creativity. To encounter any creation, even such constructions, is to encounter the spirit of its creator partially instantiated in their work.[10]

First, consider the electronic narrative as artefact. It is a commonplace that æsthetic and spiritual response are closely

---

10. Cupit, *A Critical Evaluation of Biblical Perspectives on Spiritual Development, op cit,* 151–64.

aligned. 'To some, the presence of this abstract non-physical power is strongest when contemplating natural beauty or listening to music: others feel it when they paint or create.'[11] To create is an important spiritual act. The genealogies of Cain invoke individuals who develop new modes of human creativity. From the beginning of the Old Testament cult, human creations, such as ark, tabernacle, and temple, were central to expressing, and perhaps stimulating, the desire to worship.

Some Christians struggle with spirituality vested in or channelled through artefacts. However, Bruce is so confident that 'holiness' may be transferred from object to object that he describes Paul's argument that children are made holy through their parents as: '. . . an interesting extension of the Old Testament principle of holiness by association (for example Exod 29:37, 'whatever touches the altar shall become holy')'.[12]

The Ark of the Covenant is the most clearly attested example of God working through a constructed object, though it is not unique. Despite popular superstition, the power of ark, temple, bronze serpent, or any artefact, was only as a mediator of God's presence; agencies through which God's Spirit chose to act. The ark disappeared, the temple was razed and reforming King Hezekiah smashed the serpent. Christians have recognised the Spirit's use of human artefacts in architecture, iconography, vestments, music, and so on. But spiritual influence is determined, not by the label worn by the artefact's creator, but by the creative spirit of the work.

Artists whose works express joy, a love of beauty and form, an affirmation of life and goodness, a desire to enhance human

---

11.   Alister Hardy, *The Spiritual Nature of Man: A Study of Contemporary Religious Experience* (Oxford: Clarendon, 1979), 1.

12.   Frederick Bruce, *1 and 2 Corinthians* (London: Oliphants, 1971), 69.

welfare, and so on, may, perhaps inadvertently and unconsciously, and certainly indirectly, contribute to the Spirit's work.

> The Church has always needed . . . the stimulus
> of writers, artists and others who, though not
> themselves Christians, have been voices through
> which the Spirit can speak to the churches and,
> indeed, to all men and women.[13]

Conversely, there are artefacts of the Christian community
which are ugly, mean, florid, cheap, tawdry or uninspired and,
therefore, deny the very nature of the one they claim to honour.

Artefacts can also act as channels for evil. There is an
ongoing biblical tension between the impotence of idols as
human constructions, and of evil influences which work
through their physical presence.[14] But the object need not be
religious. 'How can a child in a slum experience God? Can it
have a theophany with nothing to look at but dustbins and
brick walls . . . ?'[15] This is as true for art, music, theatre and the
like as for architecture. If children grow amongst ugly and
mean-spirited artefacts they will be influenced by that. It may
seem a long step from heathen idols to secular television but, in
so far as it reflects worship of, or reverence for, that which is
not God, the prophets would have seen parallels. Common
experience is that some art and architecture, and some
television, can impoverish, darken and oppress the human
spirit.

But electronic narratives are also language. Words, and the
concepts they convey, are central in creating and sustaining,
and also undermining, relationship to God. The nexus between

---

13. John Macquarrie, *Paths in Spirituality*, second edition (Harrisburg: Morehouse, 1993), 50.

14. J Alec Motyer, 'Idolatry', in *The New Bible Dictionary*, edited by James Douglas (London: IVF, 1962).

15. Margaret Crompton, *op cit*, 56.

truth and the Father, the Messiah and, particularly, the Spirit is a significant emphasis of the biblical record. Both prophets and apostles, and their audiences, saw their message as God's truth. 'Spiritually speaking, one can go far with nothing in one's possession except the Scriptures.'[16]

Once more, it is not the label that matters.

> Whatever does not teach Christ is not apostolic, even though St Peter or St Paul does the teaching. Again, whatever preaches Christ would be apostolic even if Judas, Annas, Pilate, and Herod were doing it.[17]

The Pentateuch includes stories and ideas from the cultures out of which the people and faith of Israel were emerging. Later, the concept of kingship, alien to tribal Israel and resisted by early prophets, is expropriated to depict the Messianic kingdom. Paul confidently quotes Greek poets and borrows Greek and Roman ideas to illustrate the gospel. Although outside the revelation to Israel, such seeking could lead to God's truth and person.

There is no chasm between 'inspired' and 'secular' words. Inspiration has always been a matter of degree, canonicity always contestable. Not all canonical books are equally valuable. A passage, collection of words, or idea does not need to be encanonned to be inspired, and, therefore, revelatory. It need only be consistent with truth God wants people to know.

But words also deceive. The scriptural association of falsehood with spiritual evil was noted earlier, deception seen

---

16. Brian Hill, 'Approaches to Teaching the Bible, Part II: Development, Evangelism and Nurture', *Journal of Christian Education*, 90 (1987): 39.
17. Luther quoted by John Goldingay, *Models for Scripture* (Grand Rapids: Eerdmans, 1994), 172.

as indicative of evil. If truth is characteristic of the Spirit of God, then error, and particularly deceit, is distinctive of forces of spiritual evil.[18] The Bible frequently refers to the destructive power of the lie. Falsehood need not contradict truth directly, only fail to reveal God's presence in the world or consistently tell a different 'world story' from the truth revealed in Scripture. It is difficult to recognise truth if you live in a society whose defining ideology, especially as represented in its narratives, misrepresents reality.

The spiritual power of words and ideas used in electronic narratives means that whether they convey truth or falsehood to children is a matter of great moment. And those words gain verisimilitude from accompanying images, which suggest one should believe what is seen. The combination of image and words has the potential to deeply influence children's spirituality.

6. Children's spirituality and electronic narratives

Children's openness to spiritual influences makes them especially vulnerable to the impacts of electronic narratives. To the extent that the spirit instantiated in the narrative is coherent with the benevolence of God, that is, the creators are prompted by God's Spirit, it will foster a positive spiritual life. To the extent that the instantiated spirit is at variance with the nature of God, that is, prompted by spiritual evil, it will be deleterious to the development of healthy spirituality. Of course, Jesus' parable of the wheat and the darnel expresses the reality. Electronic narratives exhibit both inclinations, like the human spirits that produce them. This creates a very dynamic context; not only is the narrative a complex of conflicting influences, so are children, because of their varying histories, and the contexts

---

18.   M Scott Peck, *People of the Lie* (New York: Simon & Schuster, 1983).

within which they are exposed. The same narrative will affect different children's spirits differently; the same child will be differentially affected by diverse narratives.

It is not my intention to critique the impact of particular programs on the spirituality of children; that is a matter of spiritual discernment, itself a gift, best left to those who know each child. But there are general principles which can reasonably be applied. As we see these principles played out in programs we can assess the spiritual influences at work and their likely effect upon children. This takes us beyond the popular concern about violence, explicit sexuality, and bad language, which often misses the point. The 'squeaky clean' *Brady Bunch* was one of only two programs to which I restricted my children's access.

Scripture is clear about how to differentiate spiritual good from spiritual evil, a common idea stated succinctly by Jesus: '. . . a sound tree produces good fruit but a rotten tree bad fruit. A sound tree cannot bear bad fruit, nor a rotten tree bear good fruit'. Paul applies the same imagery to differentiate whether a person was responding to the Holy Spirit, or merely being self-indulgent. James indicated that 'good' was to be attributed solely to God.

The Bible is also explicit about the nature of 'good' fruit: 'holiness' (which, far from grim wowserism, is associated with the affirmation of life and love); 'truth' and 'wisdom'; having a right attitude to God; and positive human characteristics. Most comprehensive is Paul's list: 'love, joy, peace, patience, kindness, goodness, trustfulness, gentleness and self-control'. These are not 'religious' traits but commonplace aspects of life observed in people emphatic in unbelief. If all good is sourced to God then, even when conveyed by those who deny God, its influence is a consequence of the Holy Spirit's ongoing work in those people. Whenever observed, that which exhibits the true character of God bears the signature, and does the work, of God's Spirit.

By contrast, in Scripture the work of spiritual evil is seldom clear or precise. Broad terms, like 'unclean' or 'evil', especially related to 'deceit' or 'temptation', are used, in parallel with everyday human characteristics associated with disrupted relationships with God (for example blasphemy, disobedience, idolatry), and between people (for example abusiveness, factionalism, jealousy, pitilessness); and destructive personal qualities (for example arrogance, boasting, greed, hedonism).

It is important for healthy spiritual development that children be exposed to narratives inspired by positive spirituality and helped to deal with narratives generated by destructive spirits. It is reality that all electronic narratives are a blend of both influences reflecting the internal spiritual battles of the creators of the narrative. What this means for our understanding of biblical narratives is too large a question for this paper. That the narratives are in electronic form does not change those general principles but it does change the context in crucial ways:

- enhanced plausibility of the 'message' due to the mutual reinforcement of word and image (children do believe what they see);
- compared to print, ready availability to children of all ages with less developmental constraints to limit impact on the very young;
- provision of images and ideas which would not be generated by the child's own imagination (for example horrific violence or sexual activity);
- inability of adults responsible for children to prevent exposure because of the range of contact points and the ability of the child to access without adult supervision;

- deliberate use of electronic media to exploit children (commercially and even by pædophiles).

Adults concerned for children's spiritual welfare need strategies to help children gain what is spiritually good, and develop defences against spiritual evil, in the electronic narratives to which they will be exposed.

7. Responding to electronic narratives

Adults concerned about transmission of values to their children will necessarily be concerned about the values inherent in ubiquitous electronic narratives. Though there is merit in considering how to optimise the impact of positive material, such concerns tend to centre on management of deleterious impacts. Three strategies can be implemented to counteract such influences:

- avoidance or removal of negative electronic narratives;
- counterbalancing with spiritual good;
- development of discernment.

Those responsible for children must always use discernment to evaluate what is available, not just for public 'hot button issues', but for values which differentiate Christian spirituality from that of the world, for example approval of pride, ambition, self-indulgence or irreverence. This particularly applies when the influence is too subtle to explain to the child, for instance, the assumption of materialism in many electronic narratives.

The first strategy, avoidance or removal, is commonly advocated. The worthy aspiration, that we can prevent children's exposure to spiritual evil or, if exposed, remove them from it, is unachievable. Nevertheless, some narratives are so harmful that the only responsible course is to guide children away wherever possible. To allow unmediated access to narratives asserting the validity of revenge, espousing race hatred or religious bigotry, or demeaning women or children is to become complicit in those values. But the narratives are so widely available and children so relatively free from parental control, this strategy is of limited efficacy.

The second strategy assumes that children will be exposed to injurious electronic narratives no matter how scrupulous their protector. This is counteracted by ensuring children are exposed to alternative narratives where spiritual good is at work. Whether God is acknowledged or not, these will be marked by such elements as:

- high levels of electronic and narrative crafts;
- stories which manifest truth;
- evident awareness of, and care for, the child audience;
- appreciation of the natural world and constructed beauty;
- affirmation of genuine virtue, and disapproval of immoral behaviour, even by the 'hero' of the narrative; and
- modelling of fruits indicative of the Spirit of God at work.

But there may be cause to be more specific. If a child is exposed to a particular evil influence, we can choose narratives which specifically counteract that. We may either pursue parallel but more positive electronic narratives or we may proffer alternative oral or print narratives.

The third strategy is the most difficult, but important for growth to spiritual maturity. This is to gradually help children develop sufficient discernment to recognise and understand different spiritual influences, and respond appropriately. There is value in teaching children how to identify and negate the impact of obvious evils like gratuitous violence and humiliating language, but that is not enough. Wherever possible, we need to share electronic narratives with children and, by our behaviour and words, expose the nature of the narrative and model ways to respond. That requires relationships where children feel free to discuss whatever they experience. This demands of adults willingness to expose their own success and failure to children and become vulnerable to them, but that is essential to the spiritual development of both anyway.

8. Conclusion

The dissemination of electronic narratives has not changed the basic principles of spiritual development but has altered radically the spiritual ecology of that development. Children can no longer be raised in an environment closed to narratives unacceptable to parents or their surrogates. Rather, they encounter an astonishing array of narratives, many created out of a bleak dehumanising spirituality or without concern for their impact upon immature spirits. It is easy to identify with community concern over media attitudes to violence and sexuality but a more sensitive discernment is required which penetrates the surface to the underlying creative spirit. All the crudeness of a program like *The Simpsons* should not disguise the underlying affirmation of love for the unlovely, marital fidelity despite provocation, repentance and forgiveness, and the like. We need to discern the 'Bethlehem stable' influence. And the warmth and humour of a program like *Friends* should not distract from its acceptance of irresponsibility and infidelity, and its disdain for 'less than beautiful' characters the 'friends' encounter. And here we discern the 'Venus fly-trap' influence. Values consistent with the Christian gospel lurk in the most unexpected electronic narratives, but we should not be surprised that negative influences predominate to the detriment of children's spiritual development. We need, not only to exercise discernment ourselves, but teach and model it to children.

Speaking of Evil: The Struggle to Speak No Evil When Teaching about it

Jerome W Berryman
Houston, USA

Abstract

Children's questions about pain and suffering in the world touch on the question of evil. To miss the seriousness of such questions misses an opportunity to teach about evil, but the language of evil has built-in evasions that make it difficult to confront evil when speaking about it. Four such evasions, each a form of escaping personal responsibility for evil, will be discussed to help avoid speaking evil when one means to teach how to confront and cope with it.

Children often 'ask' questions about evil despite the temptation to think that nothing *that* serious is going on. A person in early childhood may withdraw and become silent, as an unspoken lament about evil while someone in middle childhood might say 'He hurts me all the time'. In late childhood the question might become something like, 'Why do people hurt other people all the time'.

There are many difficulties about responding to such questions, but there is one part of the problem that is not often considered. It is how the language of evil itself can hide the reality of evil. One needs to be aware of this to avoid teaching evil indirectly when speaking of evil.

Four primary evasion traps will be identified and discussed to show the subtle way that the language of evil has developed to make the evasion of evil's reality easy and comfortable. Since the language of evil is biased toward evil, anyone who speaks of it needs to be on guard to struggle against evil when teaching about it.

'Evasion' is an attempt to escape notice. It is almost as if we, human beings, have conspired by means of our language to evade recognising our involvement with evil. We evade the need to constantly interpret evil's reality by thinking that it is a neutral thing 'out there' like a chair or abstract statistic, when in reality it cannot exist without us. Secondly, language helps us evade our responsibility for evil by making it easy to avoid speaking about it as a personal action. Thirdly, evil's irrationality and power is covered up by a misplaced pairing with the term 'good' to soften its horror. Fourthly, the language of abstraction and analysis enables us to avoid the feelings and the complex and systemic ordinariness of evil rather than speaking of it in narrative as a story we are part of. We will now examine each of these linguistic evasions in turn.

1. The symbolic nature of evil

The word 'evil,' which is at the centre of the language network used to speak about evil is a symbolic term so it always needs to be interpreted. This needs to be taken into consideration when speaking of evil, because the meaning shifts according to context and there is always a surplus of meaning that cannot be reduced to a simple, unchallenging noun with tamed, metaphoric content such as the 'arm,' 'seat,' 'back,' or 'leg' of a chair.

Paul Ricoeur identified the four roots in experience for the symbol 'evil' as disease, stain/blemish, filth, and fault. We shall return to these in a moment, but for now it is enough to notice that these experiences are part of the surplus meaning for the term 'evil'. The term 'evil' should, therefore, invite interpretation rather than conclude it. Ricoeur wrote in *The Symbolism of Evil* that the symbol and its interpretation are tied together and that the invited interpretation moves in a continuing circle.[1]

Interpretation moves from a pre-critical symbol, which was once 'explanatory,' to one of 'exploratory significance'[2] and 'gives rise to thought'.[3] In other words, one must take evil seriously to understand it, and the resulting understanding adds to the seriousness by which it is understood, which in turn adds to the meaning and so on. Entering this circle of continuing interpretation moves one from naivete, to levels of analysis, to a 'second naivete'.[4]

A symbolic response to the symbol of 'evil' is a strategy that is often forgotten in teaching about it, because the symbolic nature of the term 'evil,' is not fully realised. Ricoeur argued that 'Pure reflection makes no appeal to any myth or symbol; . . . but comprehension of evil is a sealed book for it; . . . Not only does the confession of sins appeal to a different quality of experience, but it has recourse to a different language, which we have shown to be symbolic through and through'.[5] Diagrams, charts, and the probabilities of cost/benefit analysis might be helpful for charting an ethical course, but the confession of sin and other liturgical, symbolic remedies are also vital to confront and cope with evil on its symbolic level.

Confronting and coping with evil symbolically deals with all four of the experiential roots. Evil as disease needs healing. Evil as a stain or a blemish, such as a birthmark, needs being made new. Evil as filth, so deeply dirty that it disgusts one, needs cleansing. Evil as fault—like a gap in a geological fault or as when something is 'my fault'—needs being made whole again.

---

1.   Paul Ricoeur, *The Symbolism of Evil* (Boston: Beacon Press, 1969), 351–2
2.   *Ibid*, 5.
3.   *Ibid*, 347–57.
4.   *Ibid*, 352.
5.   *Ibid*, 347.

All four of these experiential roots for the term 'evil' then are privations of the ideal. The liturgical remedy for these privations of health, purity, cleanness, and wholeness is to confess that these privations are present and to participate in symbolic acts such as baptism to wash one clean and make one new again or Holy Communion to restore the relationships with the self, God, and community in a redemptive way to make one whole once more. Such a liturgical response is not customary in the classroom, but its efficacy for dealing with evil at the symbolic level suggests that it needs to be part of teachers' repertory or to have access to it.

2. The evasion of personal responsibility for evil

Why is there no verb 'to evil?' Not every noun has a verbal form but it is surprising how many do. Even a noun with a very stable referent like 'table' becomes 'to table' in a meeting or the noun 'chair' can become 'to chair', as an action in the same meeting. The answer to the question is, in part, that most people do not wish to acknowledge their active involvement in evil, so the language about evil covers up this personal responsibility.

Responsibility is also evaded but in a quite different way when 'evil' is used as a modifying word, such as an adjective or adverb. When we say that a person, place, thing, or action is evil, it often signals that there is no need to show any ethical restraint or responsibility for one's reaction to it. Part of the art of teaching about evil is to acknowledge this linguistic cover-up and admit to sharing in the responsibility for evil and not responding to evil in an evil way.

3. The evasion of evil's irrationality and power: the pairing mistake

A third feature of the language of evil's cover up of evil's reality is that it softens the power and irrationality pointed to by pairing the term 'good' as the opposite of 'evil'. This is not strong enough. A better pairing word for 'evil' is 'sublime'. Pairing evil with the sublime may seem awkward at first, but this is because it is not customary. Why? Most people would rather try to tame evil with a less radical paring word to domesticate it. The term 'sublime' points to a reality that is as powerful and irrational as evil.

David Bentley Hart can be of help here to enlarge on the sublime by his distinction between it and beauty. The sublime, he has argued, is beyond the ability of language to describe (except to say how this is so). In *The Beauty of the Infinite: The Aesthetics of Christian Truth* Hart argued that the term 'sublime' is part of a kind of 'discourse of the unrepresentable', which involves difference, chaos, being itself, and what is completely other[6]. Pairing evil with the sublime, then, not only acknowledges the immensity of both terms in the pair, but it guards both from inappropriate domestication and simple disregard by common usage.

The irrational and language-surpassing quality of 'evil' was somewhat overlooked as a major theme in the history of philosophy until Susan Neiman's *Evil: An Alternative History of Philosophy*.[7] She reoriented the history of philosophy around the question of evil and traced the two major views of it in the West from the eighteenth century to the present. We need to go into this a bit more to examine the limits of language to speak of evil and its irrational nature.

For instance, one view insisted on coping with reality by 'finding order in addition to the miserable one presented by experience' and the other 'denied the reality of anything

---

6. David Bentley Hart, *The Beauty of the Infinite: The Aesthetics of Christian Truth* (Grand Rapids: Eerdmans, 2003), 43–93.

7. Susan Neiman, *Evil in Modern Thought: An Alternative History of Philosophy* (Princeton: Princeton University Press, 2002).

beyond brute appearances'.[8] Neiman's first group included Leibniz, Pope, Rousseau, Kant, Hegel, and Marx as examples. The second group was illustrated by Bayle, Voltaire, Hume, Sade, and Schopenhauer. Nietzsche and Freud did not fit into either category, because they 'maintain a sort of heroic scorn toward discussions of the subject that preceded their own, and any straws we might be tempted to clutch thereafter'.[9]

Is irrational evil all there is or is there a rationality to it that gives meaning to the pain and suffering that we experience? Neiman will not allow us to reduce this question to one of psychology. Instead, she argues that this question has to do with the limits of reason to find an answer, and yet, there is need for an answer that is reasonable. This paradox is not just frustrating, but when we keep children in mind it can become a source of hope for our teaching.

Towards the end of her book, Neiman related the irrationality of evil to children and hope:

> The principle of sufficient reason expresses the belief that we can find a reason for everything the world presents. It is not an idea that we derive from the world, but one that we bring to it. Kant called it a regulative principle—not a childish wish, but a drive essential to reason itself. Children display it more openly than adults because they have been less often disappointed. They will continue to ask questions even after hearing the impatient answer—*Because that's the way the world is.* Most children remain adamant. *But why is the world like that, exactly?* The only answer that will truly satisfy is this one: *Because it's the best one.* We

---

8.   Neiman, *Evil in Modern Thought, op cit*, 11.
9.   Neiman, *Evil in Modern Thought, op cit*, 12.

> stop asking why when everything is at it should
> be. No wonder Hegel called Leibniz's work a
> metaphysical fairytale; children are natural
> Leibnizians. In the child's refusal to accept a
> world that makes no sense lies all the hope that
> ever makes us start anew.[10]

Both points of view in Neiman's reading of philosophical history are limited, so an adequate response must involve approaching an understanding of evil that is reasonable *without* assuming that we can tame it, and we also must acknowledge that evil is *beyond* reason while we still try to understand it. This conclusion may not be satisfying, but it is, perhaps, the best that can be created using concepts and analyses.

It is the best we can do, because, 'A life that was inevitably meaningful would defeat itself from the start. Between the adult who knows she won't find reason in the world, and the child who refuses to stop seeking it, lies the difference between resignation and humility.'[11] Instead of a final meaning, we seem to be called to continue seeking, so it is the function of the teacher who teaches about evil to encourage this humility and the creative process that springs from it so that life may continue.

Beyond the limits of abstractions and analysis there is another path towards understanding evil that we have not yet examined. This is the path of narrative.

4. The evasion of evil's ordinary complexity: the failure to use narrative

We come now to the fourth and final linguistic evasion that masks evil's complexity, irrationality, and power. We often

---

10.   Neiman, *Evil in Modern Thought*, *op cit*, 320.

11.   Neiman, *Evil in Modern Thought*, *op cit*, 328.

underestimate evil's threat by trying to reduce it to analysis and abstract concepts when in fact narrative is needed to tell the whole story. Narrative does not exclude reason but invites it to interpret the irrational and overwhelming aspects of evil's story without excluding time, space, and the variety of human beings involved.

The importance of narrative for understanding ethics has been of interest amongst philosophers. Stanley Hauerwas, among others, has drawn contemporary attention to the importance of character, virtue, and story in ethical discourse[12] but I would like to approach the need for narrative to cope with evil by showing how it has been used to deal with the enormity of the Holocaust, which marked a new era in ethics for those who teach about evil.

The modern discussion about evil began with the earthquake of Lisbon in 1755, because it attracted the comments of most of the major philosophers of the eighteenth century. This conversation reached a consensus that natural disasters should no longer be attributed to God's actions. With this decision, evil retreated from the natural world into the human heart.

Auschwitz announced the end of the Lisbon age. Today, it is no longer possible to say that evil is simply located in the human heart. It is also located in a human network of ordinary people who, without being wholly conscious of it, work together to create evil. Narrative is especially needed today to acknowledge this new understanding of evil.

Elie Wiesel, himself a Holocaust survivor, refused to deal with abstractions when speaking of the Holocaust but even his use of personal narrative presented him with a dilemma. He was a 'messenger unable to deliver his message,' because the enormity of the Holocaust, as told by ordinary people's lives,

---

12. Stanley Hauerwas, *The Peaceable Kingdom: A Primer in Christian Ethics* (Notre Dame: University of Notre Dame Press, 1983).

turns the storyteller into 'a peddler of night and agony' and makes him or her an outcast, an 'other,' separated from the rest of humanity. Wiesel soon realised that he had to bear witness despite becoming an outcast, because each generation must learn from the story that shaped it. In particular, children need to know their heritage[13] but many people attempt to shield children from such evil.

In *One Generation After* Wiesel confronted this very question:

> *You are not troubled by other people's happiness?*
> *Or by the innocence of children?*
> I like happiness and I love children.
>
> *Then why do you tell them sad stories?*
> My stories are not sad. The children will tell you that.
>
> *But they make one cry, don't they?*
> No, they do not make one cry.
>
> *Don't tell me they make one laugh!*
> I won't. I'll only say they make one dream.[14]

It is from such wonder that children can begin to use their creativity to cope with evil. Wonder is the beginning of play and, while 'as-if' play allows children to try out adult roles and express their fears about evil, it is their 'what-if' play that allows them to find new ways to cope with it. Stories not only help face the pain and suffering of evil and give hope for the struggle against it, but for our time they can show the subtle way ordinary people may work together to create it, even when they do not consciously mean to. Thus, creativity can be

---

13. Elie Wiesel, *One Generation After* (New York: Avon Books (Bard Edition) 1972), 16. (Originally published by Random House, 1965).

14. Wiesel, *One Generation After*, *op cit*, 76.

focused to struggle against this new understanding of evil. To clarify what this new kind of evil involves let us turn to Hannah Arendt's *Eichmann in Jerusalem*.[15]

She told the story of Eichmann and his trial. The former Nazi did not turn out to be the monster everyone wanted him to be. He was an ordinary man who wanted the trains to run on time and helped achieve an efficient and well-organised way to dispose of the trains' cargo. He was honest, hard-working, and modest. He even enjoyed the company of the Jewish leaders he worked with to make things go smoothly. He was proud of his uniform, rank and position. He followed orders and tried to do a good job. The banality of evil screams in Arendt's narrative of this 'ordinary' person.

This scream could not be emitted from an analysis of what he did. The facts and figures leave one numb. Narrative is needed to make this kind of evil speak, and to make it known, because it is so ordinary. Neiman argued that the people who create this kind of evil are 'not mysterious or profound but fully within our grasp. If so, they do not infect the world at a depth that could make us despair of the world itself. Like a fungus, they may devastate reality by laying waste to its surface. Their roots, however, are shallow enough to pull up'.[16] I would like to add that this is true, at least, when a group of ordinary people *begin* to move towards, rather than struggle against, some great evil like genocide.

Eichman and other 'fungi,' at least at the beginning, do not begin as monsters. What is needed to cope with this kind of evil is a vital and creative appreciation for the ordinariness of evil and its overwhelming danger when ordinary people do not struggle against it in themselves and in those around them. Evil even waits quietly in ordinary religious education classes where lessons about evil are being taught. It waits to see if the

---

15.   Hannah Arendt, *Eichmann in Jerusalem* (New York: Viking, 1963).
16.   Neiman, *Evil in Modern Thought, op cit*, 303.

language we have created to talk about it will continue to be evasive or whether teachers will struggle to confront and cope with it in their ordinary lives.

5. Conclusion

It is important to be alert to the language we use when we speak of evil, because we can inadvertently teach evil even while we hope to teach about how to cope with it and reduce its presence in the world. Careful speaking about evil with children can be a very hopeful as well as a critical enterprise when one keeps this in mind.

What normal children bring to the world is a lack of numbness. They ask questions and seek stories about evil because it is there. They know evil is real, because of their own pain and suffering, but they can still play with the 'is' and 'ought' of life. They can juggle awful reality and hopeful questions to fashion new ways to understand and cope with evil. This is what can give teachers hope.

Adults, on the other hand, distinguish between the 'is' and the 'ought' of life and argue that the ontological fallacy cannot be bridged. One cannot move from a description of what 'is' to what one 'ought' to do. Children then respond, 'Why not?' There may not be a cookie for every good deed, but there is always a story for which one can seek a better ending. To help children look for that better ending, however, we must be on our guard against the evasions of evil that is built into our language.

To Such is Given the Kingdom of God: Reflections on the Childhood Religious Experiences of Saints and Mystics

Anne Hunt
Melbourne

Abstract

A discussion of the spirituality of children can surely benefit from consideration of the profound religious experiences of children who went on to be venerated as Christian saints and mystics. In this article, we shall firstly describe some of the most famous instances in the Christian tradition and, secondly, reflect on their significance for our understanding and appreciation of the potential of the child and adolescent for profound religious encounter with the divine. While the children whose experiences are recounted here are clearly exceptions and their gifts exceptional, as the church itself validates in the recognition that it has accorded to them, these exceptional children attest to the capacity for openness to the infinite and experience of the divine that is present in *all* children. Those involved in religious education, faith formation and sacramental preparation of children are encouraged to take careful note and to recognise and nurture children's capacity for deep religious experience.

1. Introduction

A discussion of the spirituality of children can surely benefit from consideration of the profound religious experiences of children who went on to be venerated as Christian saints and mystics. In this article, I shall firstly describe several remarkable examples from various periods of church history. Let the reader not be distracted by the fact that the records of these childhood experiences are very uneven in terms of their depth and detail. The witness as a whole to children's intense religious experience is very strong. Then, having described a number of cases, we will reflect on the significance of this well-attested phenomenon for our understanding and appreciation of the potential of the child and adolescent for profound religious encounter with the divine.[1]

2. Exceptional children, exceptional graces

The twelfth-century German mystic, Hildegard of Bingen (1098–1179) was born to parents of nobility, the youngest of ten children. She demonstrated a precocious spirituality from a young age, experiencing numerous visions from her earliest childhood, her first at about five years of age. When she was eight years old, her parents entrusted her to the care of Jutta of Spanheim, Benedictine abbess at the Disibodenberg monastery. Hildegard was then raised in a hermitage, and entered into religious life as a young woman. She was renowned in her lifetime for her charity, wisdom and sanctity. She was highly respected, for example, by her contemporary, Bernard of Clairvaux, Cistercian abbot and Doctor of the Church, and she exercised considerable power and influence. In later life, when she was forty-two years old, she experienced a great spiritual awakening, with a series of intense illuminations or visions, which she recounts in her now-famous masterpiece, *Scivias*. There, she explains: 'Heaven was opened and a fiery light of exceeding brilliance came and permeated my whole brain, and inflamed my whole heart and my whole breast, not like a

---

1.   We treat here saints from the Western tradition, but Eastern tradition would also evince an array of examples.

burning but like a warming flame, as the sun warms anything its rays touch'.[2]

Mechtild of Magdeburg (1210–1297), known as the 'Lord's nightingale' and the author of *The Flowing Light of the Godhead*, was one of the celebrated Beguine mystics. She had a profound visionary experience of the Holy Spirit at the age of only twelve years, and claimed that she received the greeting of the Holy Spirit daily henceforth, as well as frequent divine revelations and ecstatic visions. (She, together with the younger Beguine, St Mechtilde of Hakeborn (1241–1298), another of the great mystical writers of the Middle Ages, is thought to have influenced Dante in his characterisation of Matelda in *Purgatorio*, Cantos 27–33.) Another thirteenth century mystic, sometimes referred to as the Brabant mystic, Hadewijch of Antwerp, also had visions as child, as did Bridget of Sweden (1303–1373). In one of those visions, Bridget saw an altar opposite her bed, and, sitting above it, a woman in shining garments, holding a crown which she proceeded to offer to Bridget. Recognising the woman as the Virgin Mary, Bridget approached her, and then felt the weight of the crown as it was placed on her head. In another vision, a few years later, Bridget saw Christ crucified, who spoke to her, prompting a lifelong devotion to the passion and the wounds of Jesus.

Catherine of Siena (1347–1380), one of just three women who are honoured as Doctors of the Church and whose writings rank among the spiritual classics of the Christian tradition, was born in Siena to a relatively prosperous family, the twenty-fourth of twenty-five children. During her short life before her death at thirty-three years of age, Catherine received numerous mystical gifts, such as levitations during prayer, miraculous healings, ecstasies, and visions, including the experience of mystical death. A prolonged trance in 1370 resulted in her

---

2.   Hildegard of Bingen, *Scivias*, translated by Columba Hart and Jane Bishop (New York: Paulist Press, 1990), 59.

celebrated mystical work, *The Dialogue of the Seraphic Virgin Catherine of Siena*. From Catherine's earliest years, she experienced visions. Aged six years, she had what she would later describe as a vision of Christ: no words were exchanged; Christ smiled and blessed her. At seven years of age, Catherine vowed her virginity to Christ. She joined the Dominican Third Order at eighteen years of age and, in the course of the next three years, experienced celestial visions and conversations with Christ. In a now-famous vision, she experienced spiritual marriage with Christ, who placed a ring on her finger, visible to Catherine's eyes for the rest of her life.[3] Following this vision, Catherine adopted an apostolic lifestyle, helping the poor, the sick and the dying. In just a few years she became well-known as teacher, spiritual guide and channel of God's communication to the world.

Joan of Arc (1412–1431), renowned Maid of Orléans, who was burned as a heretic at the stake as a young woman of just nineteen years, is perhaps the most famous example of all young saints in the Western tradition, her case and her trial having caused a sensation across Europe, even in her lifetime. The records of her inquisition, which are exceptional in medieval trial records for their detail and length, recount her testimony that, from age thirteen, she experienced revelations from Our Lord through an inner voice, as well as visions of Archangel Michael, and of Saints Margaret of Antioch and Catherine of Alexandria.[4]

The French saint and Doctor of the Church, Francis de Sales (1567–1622), was the eldest of thirteen children, and demonstrated a profound religious sensibility as a child. One of the most important mystics at that same time was Pierre de Bérulle (1575–1629), whom Pope Urban VIII called the *Apostolus Verbi*

---

3.   See Raymond of Capua, *The Life of Catherine of Siena* §1.11.
4.   See *The Trial of Joan of Arc*, translated by Daniel Hobbins (Cambridge, Massachusetts/London England: Harvard University Press, 2005).

incarnati. Bérulle was esteemed as a master of spiritual life at just seventeen years of age. He later founded the French Oratory and is generally regarded as the initiator of the so-called French School of Spirituality, a powerful spiritual, missionary, and reform movement that animated the church in France in the early seventeenth century. His compatriot, Marie of the Incarnation (1599–1672), was a wife, a mother, then an Ursuline nun, and the first woman missionary to Canada. Marie recounted remarkable religious experiences as a child. In the best known of these, Christ appeared to Marie in a dream when she was just seven years old and asked her 'Will you be Mine?' It marked the beginning of what came to characterise her life and vocation, an unceasing Yes in reply to Christ's question. As an adult, aged twenty-six, she received trinitarian illuminations and experienced the trinitarian indwelling: the Father as her Father, the Word as her Spouse, the Holy Spirit as the one operative in all her activity. At twenty-eight, she experienced spousal union with Christ, the incarnate Word, and the summit of trinitarian mysticism.

In his childhood, the Redemptorist saint, Gerard Majella (1726–1755), had numerous visions of the Divine Child. In the first of these visions, Gerard saw the Child Jesus leave the arms of His mother Mary, to come to play with him, giving Gerard a loaf of unusually white bread. Gerard's remarkable experiences also included miraculous reception of Holy Communion from the Archangel Michael when Gerard was about eight years old, prompting his lifelong devotion to St Michael.

Don Bosco (1815–1888), founder of the Salesians, and among the most popular saints of modern times, experienced remarkable and lucid dreams during the course of his lifetime. At around nine years of age, he had his first and arguably most significant dream of his life. In this dream, a lady appointed him to be the shepherd of her children. It was a dream that was to prove programmatic for his whole life and vocation. In subsequent years, this dream recurred, with variations, together with other dreams, which also pointed to his mission and future work, as well as forecasting future events. Don Bosco was initially very skeptical of his dreams and only in later years did he come to believe that they came from God.

Dominic Savio (1842–1857) was a young associate of Don Bosco. Don Bosco met Dominic when the boy was about twelve years old, and was deeply impressed by the boy's piety and purity. Dominic, who died at fifteen, showed remarkable spiritual gifts as a child, including prophecy and visions. Twenty years after Dominic's death, he appeared in one of Don Bosco's dreams, accurately predicting events that were later to unfold.

Bernadette Soubiros, known as Bernadette of Lourdes (1844–1879), experienced eighteen visions of a woman at a grotto near Lourdes in France, in 1858, when she was fourteen years of age. In the last appearance, the woman identified herself as 'the Immaculate Conception', confirming a dogma promulgated by Pope Pius IX four years earlier, of which Bernadette knew next to nothing. Over the course of these visions, Bernadette experienced trances or ecstasies, and received from the Blessed Virgin both personal messages and messages for the world. Though her visions were initially greeted with controversy and skepticism, Bernadette's visions were authenticated by the church authorities in 1862.

Jacinta and Francisco Marto (1910–1920 and 1908–1919) received visions of the Blessed Virgin Mary in Fatima, Portugal in 1917. She re-appeared to them on the thirteenth day of each month for the following five months. In one of the visions (June 13), the Virgin Mary communicated what came to he known as the Fatima Secret. Not unexpectedly, the reports of their visions were also initially received with skepticism and disbelief by church and municipal authorities. After the last appearance on 13 October, and the occurrence of an extraordinary solar phenomenon which was witnessed by a large crowd, the authenticity of the visions was accepted and indeed applauded. Francisco developed a particular devotion to the Eucharist and would spend much time in prayer and adoration, including daily recitation of the fifteen mysteries of the Rosary. Jacinta was drawn to silence, penance and prayer, and in particular the contemplation of Christ Crucified. Both children died during an influenza epidemic, within a few years of their visions. Following its investigations, a Vatican committee determined that the children had lived lives of intense holiness, and the children were beatified in 2000 by Pope John Paul II, the youngest persons, apart from martyrs, ever to be beatified.

Gemma Galgani (1878–1903) of Lucca, who died in her early twenties, demonstrated extraordinary spiritual gifts as a child. Before the age of five years, she meditated on the passion of Christ, a devotion which developed into an understanding of her vocation to suffer with Jesus and to assist him in his suffering. At her first communion at nine years, she experienced mystical union with Christ. A rich visionary life followed, together with numerous mystical phenomena, including mystical locutions, the sweating of blood, and the complete stigmata, which appeared from 1899–1901, during which time, every Thursday evening through to Friday afternoon, Gemma would fall into a rapture and bleed from the five wounds of her stigmata. Her visions of and conversations with her guardian angel are particularly remarkable in the Christian mystical tradition.

Maximilian Kolbe (1894–1941) who, as an adult, was executed in Auschwitz during World War II, having offered himself in the place of another man who was to be put to death in a reprisal by the authorities for an escape from the camp, had a vision when twelve years old, at about the time of his first communion. In this vision, he saw Mary holding two crowns— a white one for purity, and red one for martyrdom. She asked him to choose and he chose both, a choice later born out in the death camps at Auschwitz. Faustina Kowalska (1905–1938) was also born in Poland, the third of ten children. When seven years old, she experienced God's call to religious life. At nineteen years of age, she experienced visions of Jesus in his Passion. As a young woman, she also experienced visions of her guardian angel and of Thérèse of Lisieux. It was Faustina who received the message of divine mercy, prompting the later development of the shrine and the movement of divine mercy, a movement which has since spread around the Christian world.

Elizabeth of the Trinity (1880–1906) demonstrated a profound sense of the divine from a very early age. As she herself explained: 'I was very fond of prayer, and I loved God so much that, even before my first Communion, I could not understand how it was possible to give one's heart to anyone else. From that time, I was determined to love Him alone and to live only for Him.' [5] A strong devotion to the Eucharist was evident from early in her life. At seven, she expressed the wish to be a nun. At twelve, she consecrated herself to Christ in a private vow of virginity. By fourteen, Elizabeth's desire was to enter Carmel: 'It was just before my fourteenth birthday when one day, during my thanksgiving, I felt irresistibly impelled to choose Jesus as my only spouse, and without delay I bound myself to Him by a vow of virginity. We didn't say anything to each other, but we gave ourselves to each other with such intense love that the determination to be wholly His became for me more final still.'[6] A very significant milestone in her spiritual development came with her First Communion. A visit

---

5. See *Reminiscences of Sister Elizabeth of the Trinity, Servant of God*, translated by a Benedictine of Stanbrook Abbey (Westminster Massachusetts: Newman Press, 1952), 11.

6. Conrad de Meester, editor, *Light, Love, Life: A Look at a Face and a Heart* (Elizabeth of the Trinity) (Washington DC: ICS Publications, 1987), 41.

by the communicants to the nearby Carmel of Dijon involved a conversation with the Prioress who told Elizabeth that her name means 'house of God'. It was the name that would prove to encapsulate Elizabeth's vocation. Within just a few years, Elizabeth was to come to a profound understanding of the mystery of the trinitarian indwelling, recognising 'the heaven in my soul' where the Trinity dwelled within her. She would grow to see her vocation in terms of being a 'Praise of Glory', an apostle of the Praise of Glory to the Trinity. Marie of the Trinity, sub-prioress at the time of Elizabeth's death, said of her: 'Truly she carried God within her. He radiated from her whole being.'[7]

There is arguably no more widely esteemed and popular a saint in modern times than Thérèse of Lisieux (1873–1897), who died from tuberculosis at the age of twenty-four years and whose short life is described in her autobiographical *Story of A Soul*, thanks to which we know much about her spiritual journey as a child. The Little Flower, as she came to be known, captured the imagination of the Christian world within a very few years following her death. Indeed, Thérèse's popularity was such that Pius X described her as the greatest saint of modern times. In her, we find an extraordinary spiritual development and mystical maturity achieved even in childhood. In his *Anthology of Christian Mysticism*, theologian Harvey Egan comments: 'it would be difficult to find a person in the Christian mystical tradition whom God had so radically purified at such an early age.'[8]

Born in France, Thérèse was the youngest of nine children. She claimed that from the age of three years she never refused God anything. A little incident from her childhood proved to be highly illuminating. She was invited to make her choice from a

---

7.   Conrad de Meester, editor, *Light, Love, Life,* 10.
8.   Harvey Egan, *Anthology of Christian Mysticism* (Collegeville Minnesota: Liturgical Press, 1991), 529.

basket filled with dolls' dresses and pretty pieces of fabric. Whereas Thérèse's sister chose one item that pleased her, Thérèse exclaimed 'I choose all'.[9] Therese herself explained that this incident summarised her life: 'I *choose all* "that You {God] will".'[10]

Even as a child, Thérèse experienced an intense desire to suffer for God. In adolescence, while contemplating the crucified Christ, she determined to remain at the foot of the cross for the rest of her life, gathering up Christ's redemptive blood in order to pour it out on needy souls, for the sake of their salvation. She came to see her vocation in active apostolic and missionary terms; it was to 'suffer for souls'.

It seems that she too dedicated herself to religious life from a very early age. From as young as nine, when her sister Pauline entered Carmel, she too wanted to enter Carmel in Lisieux. Initially refused permission, she was eventually granted permission to enter at fifteen. From the age of fourteen, she experienced what she described as 'assaults of love' that consumed her like a 'veritable flame'. She explains: 'At the age of fourteen, I also experienced transports of love. Ah! how I loved God! But it wasn't at all as it was after my Oblation to Love [in 1895]; it wasn't a real flame that was burning me'.[11]

Few of her sisters in Carmel noticed anything at all remarkable about her. Her sanctity remained hidden and unrecognised in the ordinariness of Carmelite life. It consisted not in great deeds but a great love lived out unassumingly in the day to day events and interactions of her short and seemingly very ordinary life. 'My vocation is love,'[12] she

9.   Thérèse of Lisieux, *Story of a Soul: The Autobiography of Saint Thérèse of Lisieux*, translated by John Clarke, third edition (Washington DC: ICS Publications, 1996), 27.

10.   *Ibid.*

11.   Thérèse of Lisieux, *Her Last Conversations*, translated by John Clarke (Washington DC: ICS Publications, 1977), 77.

12.   Thérèse of Lisieux, *Story of a Soul*, 185–200. See also Letter to Sr Marie of the Sacred Heart, 8 September 1896, *Her Last Conversations*, 20.

recognised. What came to be known as her Little Way was the way of unfailing love in the ordinariness and littleness of life. She explains: 'The Almighty has done great things in the soul of His divine Mother's child, and the greatest thing is to have shown her littleness, her impotence.'[13]

After her death, the Little Flower's 'Little Way' quickly become famous and exerted a profound impact on twentieth-century Catholicism, both lay and religious. Undoubtedly, Thérèse's enduring appeal and her remarkable impact on the modern Christian imagination is to be found in her genuinely childlike reliance on God alone. She herself called her way 'the little way of spiritual childhood'; it was a way that was characterised by an utterly childlike dependence on, love for, and trust in God.

3. Every child's growth in grace: reflections and challenges

There are many other accounts in the Christian tradition of profound religious experience in childhood and adolescence.[14] By no means have we recounted all known instances here. It is also pertinent to remember that not all saints, mystics and visionaries have enjoyed such extraordinary graces in child-hood. Some souls have indeed come to the heights of religious

---

13.   Thérèse of Lisieux, *Story of a Soul*, 210.

14.   See, for example, modern stories of children who are in the process of canonisation and their remarkable religious experience and holiness, in Ann Ball, *Young Faces of Holiness* (Huntingdon, Indiana: Our Sunday Visitor Books, 2004). See also some of the psychological and social studies of the spiritual lives of children, including Pulitzer Prize-winner Robert Coles, *The Spiritual Life of Children* (Boston: Houghton Mifflin, 1990); Tobin Hart, *The Secret Spiritual World of Children* (Makawao, Hawaii: Inner Ocean, 2003); Edward Robinson, *The Original Vision* (Oxford, Religious Experience Research Unit, 1977); Sofia Cavalletti, 'God and The Child', in *The Religious Potential of the Child: Experience Scripture and Liturgy with Young Children*, translated by Patricia M Coulter and Julie M Coulter (Chicago: Liturgy Training Publications, 1992), 30–46.

experience after a misspent youth (and in fact it is not uncommon for this trajectory to be narrated of male saints)! My point is that instances of very profound religious experience in childhood are not at all uncommon.

These accounts of the religious experiences of childhood from among the lives of saints and mystics, as described above, can fruitfully serve to prompt our reflections on the phenomenon of religious experience in childhood and the capacity for profound religious experience in childhood and adolescence. While the accounts of these childhood experiences are, no doubt, shaped and coloured by the religious imagination of their authors and the literary genre and religious metaphor of their time and context, these experiences are not to be dismissed a mere hagiography or pious folklore. They are not to be relegated to the periphery of our considerations regarding the experience of the transcendent in youth, as if essentially fictitious and essentially conventional hagiographical constructions that are the work of popular piety and the stuff of legend. However much these accounts of profound religious experience in childhood, including visions, are garnished with the wrappings of the religious and indeed hagiographical sentiments of their time, one senses that these accounts of religious experiences are substantially genuine and authentic, that there is a verisimilitude that is deserving of our attention and respect.

These instances of profound mystical and visionary experiences and intense holiness demonstrated in childhood clearly attest to a very significant capacity for profound openness and attunement to the divine in childhood and adolescence. At the very least, they show that religious experience and understanding is by no means alien or unnatural to childhood. Indeed, they demonstrate a remarkable capacity for insight unmediated by formal education, and for a knowledge and understanding of the Christian mysteries based on personal encounter in childhood with the divine mystery.

What is particularly interesting to note is that the childhood experiences presented here were innocent of formal theological education and were recounted with directness and simplicity, in a straightforward manner, unaffected by ideology and polemics. In an unassuming manner, they expressed an unself-conscious receptivity to what had been revealed. There is no sense of straining after the extraordinary, but rather an openness to its reception. The dominant images in these childhood experiences are of littleness and powerlessness, and of childlike dependence on and trust in God. As Elizabeth of the Trinity says of her relationship to God: 'I go to Him, like a little child to its mother, so He may fill, may possess everything, and may take me and carry me away in His arms. I think that we must be so simple with God.'[15] In these religious experiences of childhood, amidst the wrappings of the religious and hagiographical sentiments of the times, is revealed the deep wisdom to which the gospels attest and which is encapsulated in Jesus' teaching: 'Unless you become like little children you will never enter the kingdom of heaven' (Mt 18:3).

One cannot but note that more girls than boys are renowned for profound religious experiences as children. Surveying the span of Christian history, few male saints are recorded as recounting significant religious, including visionary, exper-iences in their childhood or adolescence. (Indeed, relatively few details at all are given for male saints in their childhood in comparison to female saints.) This is all the more remarkable in the light of the fact that women constitute a distinct minority in the Christian pantheon of saints. Gender is clearly a factor at play here, either in the frequency of and receptivity to the

---

15. Elizabeth of the Trinity, *I Have Found God: Complete Works II*, translated by Anne Englund Nash (Washington DC: ICS Publications, 1995), Letter 169, 111.

experience itself in childhood, or in the recounting and recording of the experience. Are boys less likely to have religious experiences as children? Are girls more likely to have their experiences recounted and recorded? A hermeneutic of suspicion might suggest the possibility that the recounting of religious experience even in childhood might be serving as a strategy to bolster the esteem with which the piety and holiness of a female saint is regarded. In other words, might such accounts be functioning, in effect, to validate her sanctity, thus mitigating against a measure of discrimination in the Christian tradition against women and a deeply ingrained suspicion of their innate capacity for authentic religious experience? In such a cultural context, male sanctity would require no such strategy.[16] Such reflection on the cultural milieu is not, however, to deny the veracity of the girls' experiences, nor to say that boys do not share these kinds of profound experience.

No culture and no society is without its biases and blindspots. In our own, one could well argue that childhood itself is under threat in various insidious and destructive ways. My hope is that, in bringing various examples from the Christian tradition of children's profound religious experience into focus, all teachers and workers in religious education and faith formation would take very careful note. Children's capacity for deep religious experience and insight, precisely in childhood, is not to be underestimated. On the contrary, it is to

---

16. For general study of the social and cultural context of sainthood, including statistical profiles of saints, see Donald Weinstein and Rudolph M Bell, *Saints and Society: The Two Worlds of Christendom, 1000–1700* (Chicago: University of Chicago Press, 1982), especially 19–72. For specific attention to the issue of gender in the accounts of religious experience in childhood, see Rosalynn Voaden and Stephanie Volf, 'Visions of My Youth: Representations of the Childhood of Medieval Visionaries', in *Gendering the Middle Ages*, edited by Pauline Stafford and Anneke B Mulder-Bakker (Oxford: Blackwell, 2001), 135–54.

be respected and indeed nurtured and its insights welcomed and treasured. The preparation for and experience of First Communion is especially to be very sensitively approached as a particularly significant moment of grace in a child's spiritual development. Admittedly, the children whose experiences are recounted above are clearly exceptions and their gifts exceptional, as the church itself validates in the recognition that it has accorded to them. But these exceptional children attest to the capacity for openness to the infinite and experience of the divine that is present in *all* children.[17] As the great twentieth-century Catholic theologian, Karl Rahner SJ, recognised, in children, precisely *qua* children, we see that orientation and openness to God, that trust and freedom that achieves perfection in the relationship which we call—and to which we are all called—being a child of God.[18] To such, indeed, is given the Kingdom of God (Mt 19:13).

---

17. Helpful resources in fostering children's spirituality include Eugene C Roehlkepartain *et al*, editors, *The Handbook of Spiritual Development in Childhood and Adolescence* (Thousand Oaks, California: Sage Publications, 2006; and Donald Ratcliff, editor, *Children's Spirituality: Christian Perspectives, Research, and Applications* (Eugene, Oregon: Cascade Books, 2004).

18. Karl Rahner, 'Ideas for a Theology of Childhood', in *Theological Investigations 8: Further Theology of the Spiritual Life 2* (New York: Herder & Herder, 1971), 33–50. Rahner writes (page 47): 'Childhood as an inherent factor in our lives must take the form of trust, of openness, of expectation, of readiness to be controlled by another, of interior harmony with the unpredictable forces with which the individual finds himself confronted. It must manifest itself as freedom in contrast to that whish is merely the outcome of a predetermining design, as receptivity, as hope which is still not disillusioned. This is the childhood that must be present and active as an effective force at the very roots of our being.'

An Understanding of Children's Spirituality as a Movement Towards a Collective Self

Brendan Hyde
Melbourne

Abstract

While much of the contemporary literature describes spirituality in terms of relationality and connectedness, many of the world's mystical and contemplative traditions, both eastern and western, have understood spirituality as involving a journey towards becoming unified with the divine. At the deepest (inwards) and widest (outwards) levels of connectedness, an individual might experience unity with 'other'. The author's research into children's spirituality in Australian Catholic primary schools suggests that, in some instances, such a movement may also reveal the emergence of a 'collective self', whereby 'self' and 'other' become one and the same. Drawing upon relevant literature from the field of spirituality, as well as the findings of the author's own research, an initial exploration of the concept of a 'collective self' is undertaken, and some implications for primary religious educators seeking to nurture the spirituality of their students through the religious education curriculum are raised.

1. Introduction

As a phenomenon which has gained considerable attention in Western culture, spirituality has generally been described in scholarly literature in terms of a sense of connectedness and relationality one may experience and express in relation to self, others, and the world, or even the cosmos. For many people, spirituality also includes a sense of connectedness to a transcendent dimension, the 'other', sometimes referred to as the Mystery at the core of the universe.[1] However, some writers have extended beyond such contemporary emphases to describe spirituality as a movement towards becoming *unified* with 'other'. Whereas connectedness implies two objects being in relationship to each other, a movement towards becoming unified with 'other' entails 'self' and 'other' becoming one and the same.[2] Based upon the author's own research investigating the characteristics of children's spirituality in Australian Catholic primary schools, this paper begins to explore an understanding of spirituality as a movement towards a 'collective self', whereby 'self' and 'other' become one and the same. In the light of this exploration, some implications for primary religious educators seeking to nurture the spirituality of their students through the religious education curriculum are raised.

The ensuing discussion on children's spirituality centres around three key terms: ultimate unity, the notion of a universal consciousness, and the concept of a collective self. Each of these is described below with reference to the author's own research into children's spirituality.

1. See Maria Harris and Gabrielle Moran, *Reshaping Religious Education: Conversations on Contemporary Practice* (Louisville: Westminster John Knox, 1998), 109.

2. For a thorough discussion on the notion of spirituality as involving a movement towards becoming unified with Other, see for example Marian de Souza, 'Teaching for Effective Learning in Religious Education: A Discussion of the Perceiving, Thinking, Feeling and Intuitive Elements in the Learning Process', in *Journal of Religious Education*, 52/2 (2004): 22–30. See also Brendan Hyde, *Identifying Some Characteristics of Children's Spirituality in Australian Catholic Primary Schools: A Study within Hermeneutic Phenomenology.* Unpublished PhD Thesis, Australian Catholic University, Melbourne.

2. Ultimate unity

It has been known for some time now that people from various religious traditions, both eastern and western, as well as people that do not profess to any particular faith tradition, are capable of apperceiving spiritual experience. Such experiences have been described, albeit inadequately, by those who undergo them as experiences of unity and feelings of oneness with everything—where mind and matter become one and the same. Various studies involving neurobiological research have identified areas of the human brain which become active when an individual apperceives spiritual experience, and this may in part explain why such experiences are not limited to practitioners of religious traditions. For example, Andrew Newberg and his colleagues have described the neurobiology of transcendence as a movement towards 'absolute unitary being', proposing the notion of unitary continuum.[3] At one pole of such continuum, a person may interact with the world and with others, but experience this interaction as something from which she or he is apart. As that person progresses along the continuum, the sense of separateness becomes less distinct, and could lead to individual experiences of unity with 'other'.

In drawing on such notions as outlined in the research described above, and in exploring the spirituality of young people in a regional setting, Marian de Souza has described spirituality as a journey towards 'ultimate unity'.[4] Such a movement can be understood to spiral through different layers of connectedness with self, others, the world and possibly with the transcendent, which generally move forwards towards wider levels, or inwards to deeper levels, but which could

---

3. See for example Andrew Newberg, Eugene d'Aquili and Victor Rause, *Why God Won't Go Away: Brain Science and the Biology of Belief* (New York: Ballantine, 2001).

4. de Souza, 'Teaching for Effective Learning in Religious Education', *op cit*, 24.

recede depending upon the particular contexts of an individual's experiences and responses. De Souza has argued that such forward and inward movement, for some individuals, has the potential to lead to the widest or deepest level of connectedness, where the individual experiences becoming one with 'other', that is, 'ultimate unity'. These conclusions support the contentions of Newberg and his colleagues that the neurobiology of transcendence is a movement towards 'absolute unitary being', when 'self' blends into 'other', and mind and matter become one and the same.

The author's own research into the characteristics of children's spirituality suggest that there were instances in which some of the children experienced this movement towards 'ultimate unity', albeit momentarily.[5] Such instances involved the children engaging with corporeal, tactile activities. The particular characteristic of their spirituality which was identified in these instances was termed *the felt sense*, and involved the children consciously drawing upon the wisdom of their bodies as a natural way of knowing. The following example of hermeneutic phenomenological writing (the text), taken from the author's own research, is indicative of this movement. The children's names have been fictionalised:

> Adam headed for the seed planting activity, while Cameron, Alicia and John made their way to the table on which were placed the 'bead creation' materials. Although the children were seated within close proximity to one another, there was no interaction between them. Each was engaged and focused upon his/her own task. They appeared to be acting with total involvement in relation to their chosen activity.

5.　　Hyde, *Identifying Some Characteristics of Children's Spirituality in Australian Catholic Primary Schools*.

Action seemed to follow upon action in a unified movement from one moment to the next. So intense was each child's concentration that after a short time, it seemed that there was a natural sense of flow being experienced between child and activity.[6] There was a sense in which each child had become less aware of the separateness between her/himself and the activity in which she/he was engaged. There was a sense in which each child had become one with the activity.

Reflection upon the above text revealed that the conscious bodily perception on the part of the children in relation to their chosen activity may have resulted in experiences of unity. This, in part reflects Thomas Merton's concept of ontological awareness—the ability to perceive with one's whole Self in a direct, concrete and experiential way.[7] In such a way of knowing, one enters the real of holistic experience in which the whole of the individual is involved—mind, body and spirit — without distinction or separation. The seeds of this type of knowing were evident in the children in the above text. The children were engaged in experiences that seemed to bridge the

---

6. American psychologist Mihaly Csikszentmihalyi describes the phenomenon of flow as a holistic sensation in which a person acts with total involvement, in which a person may often perceive little distinction between self and environment. For a detailed treatment of flow, see Mihaly Csilszentmihalyi, *Beyond Boredom and Anxiety: Experiencing Flow in Work and Play* (San Francisco: Jossey Bass, 1975).

7. See Thomas Del Prete, 'Being What We Are: Thomas Merton's Spirituality of Education', in *Nurturing our Wholeness: Perspectives on Spirituality in Education*, edited by Jack Miller and Y Nakagawa (Vermont, USA: Foundation for Educational Renewal, 2002), 164–91. See also Thomas Merton, *The New Man* (New York: Farrar, Strauss and Giroux, 1999).

divide between Self and object. For a short time, it seemed that each of the children and the activity in which they were engaged had merged into a single entity. In these holistic experiences of unity, it is possible that these children were being led to a sense of their unity with 'other' in the more cosmic dimensions—in creation, and possibly in the Transcendent. In this act of being, Merton may have said, these children had experienced something of the presence of God, for God had been present to them in the very act of their own being.[8]

3. Universal consciousness

The notion of spirituality as involving a journey towards Ultimate Unity, outlined above in relation to neurobiology, is a concept reflected in the world's mystical and contemplative traditions, both eastern and western. For example, in the Hindu tradition, a person's true nature is understood to be unified with the Brahman, the Absolute. This is reflected in Hindus speaking of 'Self' with an initial capital, refer to a person's own true nature. It is also reflected in the traditional Indian greeting, *Namaste*, which in loose translation may be rendered 'The Divine presence in me meets the Divine Presence in you. I bow to the Divine Presence in you'.[9] In the Christian mystical tradition, some such as Meister Eckhart, John of the Cross, Teresa of Avila and Bonaventure describe a mysticism of being in which one experiences union with God.[10]

---

8.   Del Prete, 'Being What We Are', *op cit.*
9.   See Marian de Souza, 'Engaging the Mind, Heart and Soul of the Student in Education: Teaching for Meaning and Connection', in *Journal of Religious Education*, 53/4 (2005): 42.
10.   For a comprehensive discussion of the Christian mystical tradition, see Oliver Davis, *God Within: The Mystical Tradition of Northern Europe* (revised edition) (London: Darton, Longman and Todd, 1988).

However, if the divine presence is at the centre of each individual's 'self', then the relationship between 'self' and 'other' is also pertinent, and renders significance not just for the transcendent 'other' but also for 'other' as encountered in both the human and non-human world, that is, the divine at the core of all existence. Although this was a key element in the thinking of Thomas Merton, it was Bede Griffiths, through his engagement in the Hindu-Christian dialogue, who expanded upon this concept, and whose work sheds light upon an understanding of spirituality as movement towards a 'collective self'. Griffiths argued that a study of the central teachings of Hinduism—the Upanishads—revealed the essence that the 'I' in the deepest centre of a person, is one with the Brahman, the source of all creation. In other words, realisation of 'self' is a realisation of union with all.[11]

A key feature of the above notion is the Hindu notion of *purusha*, the supreme Person in whom the whole universe is contained, and who fills the whole of creation. An individual person, Griffiths argued, is a conscious being, that is, a being that possesses itself in conscious awareness. But for Griffiths, every human being is a person in so far as she or he participates in the 'supreme person', the *purusha*, and in this supreme consciousness. That is to say, each person is consciousness in so far as she or he shares in this *universal consciousness*. All that a person sees, hears, perceives and knows is an effect of, as well as a participation in, the universal consciousness.

---

11. Most of the writings of Bede Griffiths express this as his central theme. For a detailed treatment of this concept, see Bede Griffiths, *A New Vision of Reality: Western Science, Eastern Mysticism and Christian Faith* (Springfield, Illinois: Templegate, 1990). See also the collected writings of Bede Griffiths in Bernard Barnhart (editor) *The One Light: Bede Griffiths' Principal Writings* (Springfield, Illinois: Templegate, 2001).

However, participation in the universal consciousness does not mean that the individual no longer exists. In the same way that every element in nature is a reflection on the one reality, so every human being is a unique centre of consciousness in the universal consciousness. And, just as no one element of nature becomes lost in the ultimate reality, no individual centre of consciousness looses its unique character. Each centre of consciousness participates in the universal consciousness and it knows itself in the unity of the one being. Griffiths maintained that this is essentially what is found in the Christian doctrine of the mystical Body of Christ. This Body incorporates all of humankind in the unity of the 'one person of Christ'.

It is the opening of the individual consciousness on the universal consciousness that Griffiths described as a movement of self transcendence. It is through contact with other selves that the individual self grows. In this way, 'self' transcends the limits of its own consciousness by contact with other form of consciousness, whether those other forms of consciousness emanate from family, friends, or the wider community, race or nation. In fact, Griffith maintained that human nature is constituted by its capacity for self transcendence.

4. A collective self

Griffiths' idea that individual consciousness grows through contact with other consciousness, and that these participate in the universal consciousness parallels closely with an understanding of spirituality as a movement towards a 'collective self', a term the author has used in his own research with children to describe the way in which, at the deepest (inward) and widest (outward) levels of connectedness, each individual 'self' becomes unified with other 'selves'.

There were two particular instances from the author's research into the characteristics of children's spirituality in Australian Catholic primary schools which may indicate the notion of spirituality as a movement towards a 'collective self'.[12] The first involved a group of ten-year old children working together to complete a jigsaw puzzle. The children had been working on various sections of the puzzle, and were now in the process of joining the segments together. The following excerpt from the hermeneutic phenomenological texts of the author's study provides an initial point of reflection upon this phenomenon:

> With the arms and hands of the different children moving across one another, and in and out of each other's way, there was a sense in which a communal space had been created for the completion of this activity. They worked together with purpose. They worked as one, each using her or his different skills and talents to complete the jigsaw. It was not long before the various sections that were being completed were ready to be attached to the original larger segment. There was some excitement as this was undertaken, accompanied by looks of pride and satisfaction.

A reflection upon the above text suggests that the collective engagement of these children in the jigsaw activity gave rise to a particular relationship that was experienced between each of the children in the group. It was a relationship of common purpose. These children had become one with each other in their unified mission of completing the jigsaw, and so became united *in* the task. Each used her or his individual talents and skills in the unified undertaking of the jigsaw puzzle. There was

---

12. Hyde, *Identifying Some Characteristics of Children's Spirituality in Australian Catholic Primary Schools*.

a sense in which these children became one body with many parts to play in the successful completion of the task (See Corinthians 12: 12–27)—the emergence of a 'collective self'. This emergence seemed to entail a movement in which each individual 'self' became unified with every other 'self' among the group of children. Every 'other'—each other child and her or his 'self'—composed this 'collective self'.

In the language of Bede Griffiths, albeit at a basic level, each child—each centre of consciousness—was involved in a movement of self transcendence, surpassing the limits of its own consciousness by contact with other forms of consciousness, emanating in this instance from the peer group. It was the opening of each child's individual consciousness to the universal consciousness. Each child—each consciousness—retained its uniqueness and individuality, yet was unified in the universal consciousness. In Christian terms, this reflects the notion of the Mystical Body of Christ, in which all Christians, although unique individuals gifted with many and varied talents are unified in, and utilise their giftedness to build up the Body of Christ.

A second instance from the author's own research which may have been indicative of the emergence of a Collective Self concerned and ten-year old girl, named Michelle, and the relationship she shared with her deceased older sister, Kim.[13] Kim had died when Michelle herself was quite young, perhaps aged about two-years old. Yet Michelle, and her immediate family, seemed to continue to experience the presence of Kim in a profound, almost sacred way. During the author's conversations with Kim in small group contexts, she shared much which shed light upon this relationship, as the following hermeneutic phenomenological texts suggests:

---

13.   Hyde, *Identifying Some Characteristics of Children's Spirituality in Australian Catholic Primary Schools*.

When asked about what really mattered, Michelle's response was immediate. 'The stuff we have of Kim left, and mum's journal which says what we think about Kim', She replied. 'When Kim died, we used to have a lot of dreams about her, and mum used to write them down in a journal . . . I also have a teddy bear that used to be hers and some ornaments that used to belong to her.'

Michelle also shared an occasion on which she had had an experience—an epiphany—of Kim after her death. When Kim was alive, the family used to holiday at Port Fairy on the Victorian coastline. When they had visited this destination on one occasion after Kim's death, Michelle described in detail how she had seen Kim walking behind them, and how this had given her great joy:

'. . . and one time at Port Fairy I saw her walking behind me . . . I was amazed', continued Michelle, 'that I actually saw her again because I was young and I thought I wouldn't see her again until I was really old and had died . . . I think she had her pink dress on, but she was like a faded cloud, sort of—she didn't look alive—it was like a spirit . . .'

Michelle's relationship with Kim could, in part, be explained by the findings of David Hay and Rebecca Nye who discovered that in some instances, the children in their research appeared to have developed a kinship between themselves and the dead.[14] They suggested that during medieval times people had

---

14. David Hay and Rebecca Nye, *The Spirit of the Child* (revised edition) (London: Jessica Kingsley, 2006).

a greater sense of kinship that extended not only across generational boundaries, but also across the boundary between the living and the dead. The living would pray for the souls of the dead, while it was hoped that the dead in turn would protect the living. Such interdependency then fostered a kinship-based sense of spirituality. However, Michelle in this author's study seemed to be aware of this kinship not simply in terms of the deceased looking after her in times of difficulty or trouble. Rather, Michelle, seemed to have a heightened awareness of the relationship between herself and her deceased sister for its own sake. Although quite young when Kim died, Michelle seemed to enjoy a profound relationship with her sister that, with the support of her family, had somewhat naturally formed. In this particular instance, the profound nature of this relationship could be conceived of as the emergence of a 'collective self'. Michelle and her family seemed to experience an intimate sense of unity with Kim that exceeded the boundary between physical life and death. Each 'self' in this relationship was unified—'self' and 'self' had become one. There was a sense in which Michelle could not be defined without reference to Kim, and in which Kim could not defined without reference to Michelle.

In the language of Bede Griffiths, the growth in Michelle's consciousness was a movement of self transcendence. She had surpassed the limits of her own consciousnesses through contact with another form of consciousness, emanating in this instance from her deceased sibling. Further, it could be argued that Michelle's immediate family formed a part of this 'collective self'. Through Kim, each of their individual selves was united as a 'collective self'. They all shared in this universal consciousness which exceeded the boundaries of physical life and death.

5. Some possible implications for religious education

The question arises then as to how religious educators, particularly those in faith based contexts, might draw upon this notion of a 'collective self' in nurturing the spirituality of their students, given that students—even those in primary school — are capable of apperceiving experiences which may lead to the emergence of a 'collective self'.

If religious educators are to nurture the spirituality of their students, then perhaps one of the first considerations ought to be an attention to the types of experiences planned for students that may nurture spirituality. The drive for achievable outcomes and competencies in the curriculum, which has impacted on religious education, has tended to place emphasis on cognition to the detriment of other facets of an individual's ontology. For example, it might be important that students' know that the church is the Body of Christ, and that this Body is made up of many parts. But such knowledge may not have a lasting impact upon the learner unless it has touched the core— the soul. An experience of what it means to be one Body with many parts may have a more lasting impact. Can the emergence of a 'collective self', given that such an emergence is possible, be drawn upon in the religious education classroom? The answer is in the affirmative, and it is possible to plan within the curriculum experiences which may give rise to the emergence of a 'collective self'.

Activities and experiences which may enable the notion of a group spirit to emerge may also facilitate the emergence of a 'collective self'. These could, of course, include small group tasks which may engage the students in such a way that each contributes her or his particular talents towards the completion of the task, such as the jigsaw activity referred to in this paper. Most subject areas within the curriculum can include activities of this nature. As well, many of the trust exercises and team building undertakings advocated by educators such as Rachel

Kessler and Sue Phillips may also facilitate the emergence of a 'collective self'.[15] Such activities are valid. In Griffith's language, they enable centres of consciousness to grow through contact with other centres of consciousness.

However, given the catechetical nature of many religious education programs in Australia, could, for example, the invitation (stress *invitation*) to communal prayer provide possible instances in which a 'collective self' could emerge? Could the invitation to be involved in meaningful liturgy similarly give rise to the emergence of a 'collective self'? And, is it possible to give adequate attention to the preparation of the space in which such rituals are to occur? For example, the dimming of lights, the placement of furniture, the use of candles and sensory stimuli such as an oil burner, music, and the like, may contribute to a shared space—a sacred space— which may be conducive to the emergence of a 'collective self'. These experiences, in which people gather as one Body united in Christ, have the potential to enable the individual's cons- ciousness to transcend the limits of its own consciousness by contact with other forms of consciousness which have gathered to unite in heart and mind to celebrate the presence of Jesus as the risen Christ.

All of this represents an initial exploration, and further reflection upon the findings of the author's own research. The emergence of a 'collective self' among children of primary

---

15. American educator Rachel Kessler, as well as British educator Sue Phillips, advocate activities of this nature. See for example Rachel Kessler, *The Soul of Education: Helping Students Find Connection, Compassion and Character* (Alexandra: Association for Supervision and Curriculum Development, 2000). See also Sue Phillips, 'The Theatre of Learning: Developing Spirituality through Experiential and Active Techniques which also Promote Academic Achievement in Religious Education', in *International Handbook of the Religious, Moral and Spiritual Dimensions in Education*, edited by Marian de Souza *et al* (Dordrecht, The Netherlands: Springer, 2006), 1377–1389.

school age is possible. Questions in relation to how religious educators might draw upon the notion of a 'collective self' as a means of nurturing the spirituality of their students is an area requiring further investigation.

Spirituality in Education: Addressing the Inner and Outer Lives of Students to Promote Meaning and Connectedness in Learning

Marian de Souza
Ballarat

Abstract

Statistics and anecdotal evidence reflect the fact that many young people appear to experience disillusionment and a sense of hopelessness and disconnection and that they contribute to the rising statistics of mental health problems in Australia. Further statistics regularly indicate the growing indifference of young people to the traditional institutions, such as religion, that in previous years may have offered some hope, meaning and purpose. Instead, for contemporary young people, their longing and searching takes place in spaces without boundaries which could be unsatisfying and sometimes, dangerous. Alternative sources and channels need to be investigated that may provide credible frameworks within which young people may continue their search.

This paper investigates the spirituality factor in education and argues that by addressing both the inner and outer lives of students there is a greater chance of promoting balance and wellbeing for students and their communities. It then proposes an arts approach that will draw on the culture and wisdom of different religious traditions to help young people develop their individuality or to take a side step in order to view the world from a different perspective in an attempt to find meaning and connectedness in their lives.

1. Introduction

In recent years, the rising statistics that indicate levels of depression and other mental health problems amongst our young, including primary school going children, should be of real concern to Australians.[1] An attempt by the Federal Government to address some of these concerns has been to introduce and fund a values education program for all Australian schools. As a result of the early stages of the research, nine values were identified as core values and subsequent stages of the research have encouraged some excellent practices in introducing and raising awareness of these values in many schools.[2]

However, in contemporary Australia, it will not be surprising that some problems may emerge when an attempt is made to identify nine Australian values that are intended to be core values across the existing multicultural and multi-faith environment with the expectation that these values may be interpreted and practised with the same consistency amongst all Australians. In the consumer-driven culture that most children grow up in today, the values that they are exposed to through the media, and indeed, in some of their communities, may well be ones that we do not wish to promote: money and success at all costs, personal attacks on politicians as a strategy to win points, the attitude of some males in the sporting arena towards women and so on. As Popov contends, the word

---

1. For instance, see Youth Survey Mission Australia (2002), *2002 Mission Australia Youth Survey Results*. At <http://www.missionaustralia.com.au/cm/Resources/SocialPolicydocs/SPR08_Youth%20Survey.pdf>. (Accessed 7 November 2003).

2. For more information about values education in Australia go to the following website: <http://www.valueseducation.edu.au/values/>.

'virtues' is a more appropriate one to use in the educational context as virtues may always be seen as positive things.[3]

This article offers the argument that positive values may be seen as expressions of the relational dimensions of the individual, that is the connected self (outer persona) feels to 'self' (inner persona) and everything that is other than 'self'. Further, a proposal is put forward that a framework needs to be developed within which selected values can be authenticated. For instance, in religious schools, values are derived from the religious teachings within which the philosophical approach to education may be embedded. Thus, in Christian schools, the term 'gospel' values take on a particular meaning. They refer to values taught and modeled by Jesus Christ which have been passed on through the New Testament, the sacred book of Christians and which have become the basis for Christian living.

Conversely, in a secular educational system, residing as it does in a pluralist social context where relativity has become an important consideration, any attempt to define certain values as being somewhat 'more' than other values becomes complex and, perhaps, unattainable. One way forward is to develop an educational approach that addresses the spiritual dimension of students' lives and, given the wide use of the term spirituality in several fields and disciplines, it is necessary to describe its interpretation as it is used in this paper.

Spirituality, here, is recognised as an innate and essential element of every person. This understanding informed a small research study that examined the perceptions and expressions of the spirituality of sixteen to twenty year olds and whose

---

3.   Linda Popov suggests the use of the word 'virtues' instead of 'values' and outlines her reasons for this in *The Virtues Project Educator's Guide: Simple Ways to Create a Culture of Character* (Canada: Jalna Press, 1998).

findings have been reported elsewhere.[4] However, to clarify the understanding of spirituality as it is used in this article, a brief explanation follows.

In our research study, we found that the young people who had chosen to participate showed a strong sense of connectedness to at least one other person. For most, it was one or both parents, their siblings, and their friends. In a few cases, it was just one parent or a grandparent. For one young man it was his mother and his five-year old daughter. Within these relationships, most of the participants perceived themselves to be caring people who would stand up and protect those they cared about. We found that as we discussed the possibility of relationships to wider circles within the local and global community, most of these young people had little sense of connectedness to those who did not belong to their immediate circle. They could not identify with or feel compassion for those who were different. (Please note, the study was conducted during the time of the 'Children Overboard' affair in Australia and many of the participants tended to use the language of the media and politicians, such as, 'boat people', 'dole bludger', 'queue jumpers' and so on.) However, there were two individuals who clearly did identify and empathise with people who were different, for instance, the people who had arrived on Australian shores to seek refuge, and they provided reasons why they felt as they did. What was of more interest was the fact that there were two more individuals who showed little connectedness to the refugees in their immediate response, and then back-tracked to say, 'but we should feel something'.

We interpreted the different responses as indications of a spiritual maturity. Thus, two individuals had a spiritual

---

4.   See Marian de Souza, Patricia Cartwright and EJ McGilp, 'The Perceptions of Young People Who Live in a Regional City in Australia of Their Spiritual Wellbeing: Implications for Education', *Journal of Youth Studies*, 7/2 (2004): 155–72.

maturity that was expressed in connectedness to a wider communal circle than most of the other participants who were only closely connected to people within their immediate circle. Accordingly, we understood the two responses which expressed a certain level of discomfort in not being able to connect with or empathise with Other who was different as an indication that these individuals were moving towards a spiritual maturity.

Spirituality, then, could be described as pertaining to the relational dimension of being which is reflected in expressions of connectedness that spiral outwards to link with the social, communal and physical 'other'. We also recognised that engaging with or learning about 'other' promoted self knowledge, that is, there is a corresponding inward movement towards knowledge of self. Such an understanding reflects Merton's concept of 'original unity'[5] where 'the process of inner transformation that leads to self-discovery is simultaneously a process of discovering our deep relatedness to other[s]' and vice versa.

Consequently, human expressions that reflect these layers of connectedness may be recognised as expressions of spirituality where, at the deepest and widest level, 'everything forms a single whole'[6] and 'self' merges with 'other'. This could take over a lifetime to emerge so that I describe human spirituality as a journey towards 'ultimate unity'.[7] This also supports

---

5.   Cited in Thomas Del Prete, 'Being What We Are: Thomas Merton's
      Spirituality in Education', in *Nurturing our Wholeness: Perspectives on
      Spirituality in Education*, edited by Jack Miller and Yoshida Nakagawa
      (Rutland, Vermont USA: Foundation for Educational Renewal, 2002),
      164–92.

6 . Pierre Tielhard de Chardin, *The Divine Milieu* (New York: Harper and
      Row Publishers, 1960), 61.

7.   For a more detailed discussion of this concept see Marian de Souza,
      'Contemporary Influences on the Spirituality of Young People:
      Implications for Education', in *International Journal of Children's*

Newberg's discussion of the neurology of transcendence as a movement towards 'absolute unitary being', that is, when the Self blends into other and mind and matter become one and the same; that is, Newberg describes the human person on a 'unitary continuum'. At one end, the individual interacts with 'other' in their community and in the world but experiences this as something from which s/he is apart. However, as s/he moves along the unitary continuum, the lines of separation become blurred until s/he reaches the point of 'absolute unitary being'.[8]

Thus if we understand spirituality as pertaining to a relational dimension of being which is built up with layers of connectedness, it has a distinct relevance for the development of learning programs that address this aspect of a student's life. Certainly, expressions of connectedness should reflect positive values which are foundational to all meaningful, transformational learning. As well, these connecting layers should transcend religious, social, cultural and political landscapes and boundaries although the expressions may, indeed, be influenced by such factors. It is the layers of connectedness that individuals experience that lead them to a discovery of a sense of *self* and *place* within their communities and the wider world, and ultimately, help them to find *meaning* and *purpose* in their lives.[9]

Spirituality, 8/3 (2003): 269–79 and Marian de Souza, 'The Role of the School and Educational Programs in Nurturing the Spirituality of Young People', in *At the Heart of Education: School Chaplaincy and Pastoral Care*, edited by James Norman (Ireland: Veritas Publications, 2004a), 122–33.

8.   See Andrew Newberg, Eugene d'Aquili and Victor Rause, *Why God Won't Go Away: Brain Science and the Biology of Belief* (New York: Ballantine, 2001), 145.

9.   For more discussion see Marian de Souza, 'Growing Empathetic, Compassionate, Meaningful and Hopefilled Students: Re-discovering the Spiritual Dimension in Education', in *New Horizons in Education*.

2. An approach to learning

Elsewhere, I have proposed a learning approach which addresses the intellectual, emotional and spiritual dimension of being and which engages the following elements: perceiving and sensing, thinking, feeling and intuiting.[10] This paper will focus on one element in this learning process: Intuition. It will examine various theories about intuition and discuss its relevance to the learning process.

What is significant in the process of this learning approach is that it addresses both the *inner* and the *outer* lives of the student where learning begins at the surface of the conscious and unconscious mind, that is conscious and unconscious perceptions are absorbed through the senses. These perceptions generate thoughts and feelings within the conscious mind, or from the subconscious mind which, in turn, may trigger memories, or 'gut-feelings' which rise from a depth level within the unconscious mind. Such feelings appear to connect with and be prompted by the individual's tacit knowledge[11] Polanyi describes this as learning without awareness:

> Thus, in the structure of tacit knowing, we have found a mechanism which can produce discoveries by steps we cannot specify. This mechanism may then account for scientific

Volume 113, (2005): 41–52 and also Marian de Souza, 'Teaching for Connectedness and Meaning: The Role of Spirituality in the Learning Process', in *Panorama. International Journal of Comparative Religious Education and Values*, 16/ Summer/Winter (2004b): 56–70.

10. See Marian de Souza, 'Teaching for Effective Learning in Religious Education: A Discussion of the Perceiving, Thinking, Feeling and Intuiting Elements in the Learning Process', in *Journal of Religious Education*, 52/3 (2004c): 22–30.

11. See Michael Polyanyi, *The Tacit Dimension* (New York: Anchor Books, 1967) and Michael Polyanyi, *Knowing and Being: Essays by Michael Polyanyi* (London: Routledge & Kegan Paul, 1969).

intuition, for which no other explanation is known so far . . .

We have seen *tacit knowledge* to comprise two kinds of awareness, *subsidiary awareness* and *focal awareness*. Now we see *tacit knowledge* opposed to *explicit knowledge*; but these two are not sharply divided. While tacit knowledge can be possessed by itself, explicit knowledge must rely on being tacitly understood and applied. Hence all knowledge is *either tacit or rooted in tacit knowledge*. A *wholly* explicit knowledge is unthinkable.[12]

Accordingly, the approach to learning we are discussing here, recognises that knowledge which has been gained implicitly through unconscious perceptions can produce the 'gut-feelings' which may result in an intuition. Such an intuition may spring into the conscious mind and, perhaps, lead to transformed conscious thinking and action, thereby raising the potential for the learning to become vital, meaningful and transformative for students regardless of their background. It is these features which engage both the inner and the outer lives of students, at the levels of head, heart, soul and senses, and they provide avenues of connectedness and meaning in the learning process so that the intellectual, emotional and spiritual dimensions of education are addressed. Potentially, then, the process may provide students with a sense of self and place within their communities which, in turn, should generate different levels of meaning and purpose in their lives.

Most educators will be able to recall inspired moments of effective learning during their professional experience and if such experiences were analysed, it is more than possible that the findings would indicate that students had been engaged at

---

12. Polanyi, *Knowing and Being, op cit*, 144.

intellectual, emotional and spiritual levels even though teachers had not quite planned for or articulated these things. Student characteristics that could be described at such moments would include interest and enthusiasm, concentration, absorption and immersion in a particular activity resulting in insightful, creative, enterprising, exciting initiatives or outcomes. Csikzentmihalyi described such an experience as the optimal experience based on the concept of 'flow' which occurs when an individual's mind and body are so involved in an activity that nothing else seems to matter and no other distracting thoughts or anxieties can intrude. Instead, the whole of their being is directed at the achievement of the goal and consciousness becomes 'harmoniously ordered'. Achievement of the outcome, then, is dependant on their own ability and creativity and is experienced when there is *'order in consciousness'* which occurs 'when psychic energy—or attention—is invested in realistic goals, and when skills match the opportunities for action'.[13]

It is a contention of this paper that this process of 'flow' describes the experience whereby the individual is so deeply focused and connected that s/he becomes one with the activity with which they are engaged. A further useful feature of the learning approach discussed here will promote opportunities for students to enter the 'flow' experience that Csikzentmihalyi has described.

In general, the elements of perceiving, thinking and feeling are foundational to most learning programs although with varying emphases given to each. For instance, most learning programs are heavily weighted in favour of the cognitive domain where different levels of thinking and rational learning are strongly supported. It is only in recent years, since the literature on emotional intelligence has become more readily

---

13. For a more detailed discussion of 'Flow' see Mihaly Csikzentmihalyi, *Flow: The Classic Work on How to Achieve Happiness* (London: Rider, 1992, 2002), 6.

available, that the role of the emotions in learning and emotional literacy is beginning to attract attention. Again, in the highly visual world we live in, usually more consideration is given to the use of visual stimuli, and to a somewhat lesser degree, the use of aural stimuli with much less focus on the other senses. Thus, the role of implicit or unconscious learning through different senses which lead to tacit knowledge has often been overlooked. Consequently, the role of intuitions or intuitive thinking has largely been ignored in primary and secondary education, and it is this element and its implications for engaged and transformative learning that I would like to explore further in this paper.

3. The role of intuition in the learning process

To begin with, intuitive thinking has been perceived as springing from deep within the individual's psyche which presents her/him with an instant and clear understanding of the phenomena or a solution to a problem, but it is not quite clear what the process is or what prompts such a response.[14] Generally, intuitive responses appear to promote enhanced understanding of a situation by presenting the whole rather than the part which assists the rational and logical mind to arrive at a conclusion. In other words, it plays a complementary role.

---

14. For various discussions on intuition see Guy Claxton, 'The Anatomy of Intuition', in *The Intuitive Practitioner: On the Value of Not Always Knowing What one is Doing*, edited by Terry Atkinson and Guy Claxton (Buckingham, Philadelphia: Open University Press, 2000) 32–52; Michael Eraut, 'The Intuitive Practitioner: A Critical Overview', in *The Intuitive Practitioner, op cit*, 255–68 and James Hillman, *The Soul's Code: In Search of Character and Calling* (Australia: Random House, 1996), 97–101.

Marian de Souza

This is clarified by Myers[15] who asserts that the human person has the ability to learn in two ways, consciously or explicitly, and unconsciously or implicitly. He argues that the idea in contemporary psychological thinking is that 'most of our everyday thinking, feeling, and acting operate outside conscious awareness' which is a difficult concept for most people to accept since 'our consciousness is biased to think that its own intentions and deliberate choices rule our lives'. As Myers explains, this is not surprising since our conscious minds tend to focus on the visible self, however, he draws on contemporary research to assert that at lower and deeper levels, 'the mind is buzzing with influential happenings that are not reportably conscious'. He cites Wegner and Smart who describe this subterranean world as 'deep cognitive activation' which allows us to implicitly or intuitively recall things that we cannot explicitly remember. It is Myer's contention that these two ways of knowing, rational and intuitive, are parallel processes and he refers to the process aligned with the intuitive way of knowing as 'thinking lite', claiming that it requires 'one-fourth the effort of regular thinking':

> Our minds process vast amounts of information outside of consciousness, beyond language. Inside our ever-active brain, many streams of activity flow in parallel, function automatically, are remembered implicitly, and only occasionally surface as conscious words.

This notion that intuitions are another way of knowing is implicit in the way Hillman describes the intuiting process when he says it is the 'traditional model of perceiving the

---

15. See David G Myers, *Intuition: Its Powers and Perils* (New Haven and London: Yale University Press, 2002), 15, 23, 29.

invisible'[16] and that a person can have an intuition 'without any known process of cogitation or reflective thinking'. Hillman claims that intuitions occur without any conscious effort on our part. They come 'as a sudden idea, a definite judgement, a grasped meaning . . . rapid understanding . . . the "aha *Erlebnis*", that gasping response of sudden insight'. The other characteristics, according to Hillman, are the suddenness and the mystery with which an intuition can occur, when suddenly one perceives the whole rather than the part without having any explanation of how it happened.

Hogarth also notes this characteristic of an intuition, the lack of awareness of how outcomes—or judgments—have been achieved.[17] Hogarth sees intuitions as 'mysterious'—somehow producing a solution without the use of a 'conscious' process. Here, once again, is a reference to a non-conscious process, thus supporting Myer's contention. Indeed, Myers uses the term *'nonconscious learning'* for 'what you know, but don't know you know, (which) affects you more than you know'[18] which is an apt description for tacit knowledge as identified by Polanyi, that is, knowledge that we have but we are unable to explain how we have it. It is knowledge that has been absorbed unconsciously or implicitly through our senses and stored in our unconscious minds. It was Polanyi's contention that a person's interest and curiosity led them to acts of discovery and creativity which contradicted the dominant position of the day that science was somehow value-free.[19] Accordingly Polanyi 'sought to bring into creative tension a concern with reasoned

---

16. Hillman, 1996, *op cit*, 97, 98.
17. See RM Hogarth, *Educating Intuition* (Chicago and London: University of Chicago Press, 2001), 7.
18. Myers, *Intuition. Its Powers and Perils*, *op cit*, 51.
19. Polanyi, *The Tacit Dimension*, *op cit*.

and critical interrogation with other, more 'tacit' forms of knowing'.[20]

In recent years, the role of the intuitive process in effective decision making has been acknowledged in fields of business and other work environments[21] where it has been found that the more experienced a person is, the more s/he is able to, intuitively, make good decisions or arrive at suitable solutions to problems. This finding suggests that intuitions spring from the tacit knowledge that people have accumulated implicitly over a period of time so that, at an unconscious level, they recognise similarities between one situation and others they have experienced previously. This helps them to 'read' the new situation with insight and find appropriate answers.

Hogarth clearly articulates his perspective on intuition through the dimensions of process, content and correlates.[22] He supports this contention in a discussion of five key ideas.[23] Firstly, that the human person is one organism with many information processing systems. Secondly, all learning is shaped by experience. Thirdly, the human person has two systems for learning and doing. Fourthly, expertise is foundational to intuitive responses, and fifthly, he offers a process whereby scientific method can be made intuitive. These ideas do support the views presented earlier, that is, intuitions result

---

20. For a more detailed discussion of Polanyi's concept of tacit knowledge see Mark K Smith, 'Michael Polanyi and Tacit Knowledge', *The Encyclopedia of Informal Education*, 2003, www.infed.org/thinkers/polanyi.htm (accessed 19th February, 2005).

21. See B Breen, 'What's Your Intuition?', *Fast Company*, Issue 38, September 2000, 290. See <www.fastcompany.com/online/38/klein. html> (accessed 12 May 2004) and J Mara, J & Associates, 'Intuition: Trusting your Gut', *Australian Institute of Banking and Finance, Professional Development* (14 August 2002, NSW) at <www.intuitivethinking.com.au> (accessed 20 February 2005).

22. Hogarth, *Educating Intuition, op cit*, 7.

23. Hogarth, *Educating Intuition, op cit*, 14.

from unconscious perceptions which are processed differently to conscious perceptions. Hogarth refers to these two systems of learning and doing as *tacit* and *deliberate*. Secondly, he discusses the role of experience and the levels of domain-specific expertise in intuitive responses which support the assertion by Breen[24] and Mara[25] that people with experience and who have built up their expertise in a particular field are more capable of making effective, intuitive decisions in those fields.

Keeping in mind that intuitive learning is an unconscious process, it is interesting that Hogarth offers a framework whereby intuition can be educated.[26] He suggests that attention must be given to the environment where the learning may take place since tacit learning is reactive. Therefore, if the environment is 'kind' or 'wicked' different intuitive responses will be learned, and not all these will be appropriate. The term 'kind' is used to describe learning structures where people receive good feedback, connections are made, and the right lesson is learned from experience. In a 'wicked' learning environment, feedback can be misleading, connections can be misconstrued so that the right lesson is not always learned, for instance, human experience in the past led people to intuitively believe the world was flat.

Secondly, Hogarth stresses the importance of appropriate feedback and reinforcement since it affects both the tacit and the deliberate systems but advises the need for caution. Thus, when the environment is kind, the automatic processing of feedback is critical and functional but in a wicked environment, the feedback may be faulty which could lead to delays, random disturbances and other confounding factors. For instance, Hogarth points out that the process that leads to the acquisition of valid beliefs about the world is the same process that leads to

24. Breen, 'What's your Intuition?' *op cit.*

25. J Mara, J & Associates. 'Intuition: Trusting your Gut', *op cit.*

26. Hogarth, *Educating Intuition, op cit,* 207

the acquiring of superstitions. In order to avoid faulty intuitive responses, Hogarth suggests a third factor in his framework: imposing circuit-breakers. By this he means that the *deliberate system* should be used to censor automatic reactions. Thus, rational thinking is brought into partnership with intuitive thinking. Another factor that Hogarth identifies is that connection is an effective learning mechanism. He suggests that learning through narrative mode is particularly effective since it encourages people to make connections more easily than they would if they used logical modes of thinking. Hogarth recognises the role of the emotions as foundational to all learning, particularly, when the process of learning requires making a choice which can lead to conflict. Finally, Hogarth argues that the scientific method of rules and reasoning can be made intuitive by moving through the process of deliberation to experience. Likewise, he highlights that while the tacit system is based on experiential learning, it can become limited. Therefore, it needs to work in conjunction with the deliberate system.

Wilber[27] (2000, 2001) provides another way of under-standing perceptions and intuitions which he links to the learning process. He proposes an integral vision or approach which is a 'judicial blend of ancient wisdom and modern knowledge'[28] and recognises a *spectrum of human consciousness* which discloses to each individual, a different type of world.[29] That is, each person's perceptions will reveal a different perspective of the same object or situation depending on their circumstances, background, cultural and religious influences and so on. In Wilber's words:

---

27. See Ken Wilber, *The Eye of Spirit: An Integral Vision for a World Gone Slightly Mad* (Boston and London: Shambhala. Publications Inc, 2000, 2001), 34.
28. Wilber, *The Eye of Spirit, op cit*, 7.
29. Wilber, *The Eye of Spirit, op cit*, 76.

Put in its simplest form, there is, at the very least, the eye of flesh, the eye of mind, and the eye of spirit (or the eye of contemplation). An exclusive or predominant reliance on one of these modes produces, for example, empiricism, rationalism, and mysticism . . . each of these modes of knowing has its own specific and quite valid set of referents: *sensibilia, intelligibilia, and transcendelia.*[30]

Wilber argues that all valid knowledge has the following components or strands: *instrumental injunction; intuitive apprehension, and communal confirmation.* The first implies that if you want to know something you have to do it—the action and/or experience. The second refers to the 'immediate experience of the domain disclosed by the injunction.' This is the direct grasping of the information that has been produced by the experience whether it is sensory experience, mental experience or spiritual experience. The third component relates to checking or validating the findings or results with others who have already successfully completed the first two components. Wilber's second strand appears to be a link to intuitive learning as it is being discussed here, however, a detailed discussion of Wilber's integral approach is beyond the scope of this paper.

It would seem, then, from these understandings of intuition that there needs to be some recognition of its significance in the learning process, and indeed, an acceptance of different levels of consciousness which promote deep and transformative learning and which will involve the inner and outer lives of the learner. Such a process requires learning activities that help

---

30. *Ibid.*

students connect new learning with previous learning at both conscious and unconscious levels; that provide a balance between movement and stillness; that recognise the need to move between acceptable levels of working noise and silence; that encourage social interaction between groups of students and inner reflection; that promote variation between instruction and discovery modes of learning. Such a process, in fact, may run counter to the current trend of busy timetables and crowded curricula in many schools where there is pressure for all students to achieve particular outcomes, and where the focus is on cognition and knowledge that relates to the outer lives of students. More attention needs to be given to the intuitive learning processes and responses that may accompany the thinking and feeling processes and which may generate deeper and more meaningful learning.

4. Application

An important aspect of this learning approach relates to the planning of units of work, or particular lessons. Teachers need to consider the different dimensions of learning that may be experienced in their classrooms, which includes conscious and unconscious learning. In the current system, units of work are planned around stated outcomes related to the achievement of knowledge and skills that students are expected to demonstrate at the end of the unit or lesson. The achievement of these cognitive outcomes provide a useful source of measurement for the teacher which can be an indication that the learning has been successful or otherwise. However, it is possible, in some instances, that students will be able to provide 'correct' answers without any deep or transformative learning having taken place.

Sometimes, in the current system, there may be an articulation of affective learning outcomes in relation to values and attitudes and these may also be used to provide some kind of assessment in terms of participation and a display of interest. However, assessment of affective learning outcomes can be problematic in terms of accuracy and subjectivity. Instead, self-assessment strategies would be more useful for affective learning since these promote self-reflection as students are encouraged to consider what they have learnt, whether it has been interesting or challenging and so on. This process also assists the child to become more connected with their inner selves and to get to know who they are. Finally, in the current system, it is highly unlikely that learning outcomes that address the spiritual dimension of learning will be articulated so that the role of activities that address inner reflection and implicit learning is not recognised efficiently.

Given the above situation which is reflected in many classrooms, the learning approach I propose incorporates these three types of learning outcomes, cognitive, affective and spiritual, the first two dealing with knowledge, skills and feelings, and the latter providing an integrating role through inner reflection and intuition. When attention is given to the complementarity of each of these elements, the learning process should become a transformative experience. This approach does not require that affective and spiritual learning outcomes should be measured. Rather they should be planned for so as to ensure that learning moves from the surface to deeper, transformational learning.

In order to achieve these things it is absolutely essential that appropriate resources are selected which may connect to and elicit the tacit knowledge that students have accumulated. Such resources should be aimed at triggering responses through all the senses so that students are able to access the stimuli at different points to produce a variation of perceptions. In addition, there needs to be time built into the learning process to allow the students to reflect or dwell on the stimuli in order for connections to be made at a depth level where thinking, feeling and intuiting generates a complementary response. In turn, the sharing of these perceptions amongst class groups may promote feelings and intuitive responses from other students as some memory within them resonates and connects with the other.

One approach that may be valuable in addressing these three dimensions in learning is the use of the arts as stimuli to promote learning across the curriculum. For instance, I use an illustrated story to teach the effects of littering. I tell the story of *The Death of a Wombat*[31] with appropriate images on power-point slides and music playing to provide a backdrop to the story. The images will depict the beauty of the natural bushland, images of some of the flora and fauna that are found there, and images of a wombat going about its daily business. As the story unfolds, I use an image of an empty bottle lying on the ground at the edge of the bush (the implications being that it has possibly been thrown from a passing car). And eventually there are some images of a bushfire and its aftermath with the story telling of the death of the wombat.

At the end of the viewing/listening, there should be some silent time. Carefully worded questions follow to prompt deep thinking from the students about the progression of events that come from a bottle being thrown out of a car window. Further questions ask students to reflect on times they have been guilty of littering, even if it was only a small piece of litter. Students are asked for creative responses to the story to reflect their thoughts and feelings. Other learning activities around the topic will flow on from this session. The significance of such a session is that students are taking in many different things at the same time but only some of these are through the conscious mind. Listening to the story is at the conscious level; the images and music, however, are being absorbed through different senses

---

31. Ivan Smith, *The Death of a Wombat* (Melbourne: Wren Publishing, 1972).

and, as such, they convey other sensations, ideas and feelings, many of which are being processed at an unconscious level. However, at the end of the session, when students are required to answer questions or develop a creative response, both the conscious and unconscious learning will, together, generate their responses.

While this approach may be confronting to teachers since there is pressure to find innovative and stimulating resources and activities to present and communicate the lesson's content which will seriously engage and challenge their students, the enrichment of learning that follows should provide the motivation to continue. Learning, then, engages the head, heart, soul and senses and has the potential to have a more lasting impact, something that the children may be able to revisit throughout their lives and the learning experiences should provide those moments that both teachers and students remember as enjoyable and meaningful.

5. Conclusion

As I have suggested before,[32] more activities that draw on the inner self and involve creativity, imagination, story-telling, reflection and contemplation, stillness and silence should be explored and trialled to evaluate their effectiveness in addressing the three dimensions, cognitive, affective and spiritual. Daily timetables and classroom structures should be investigated and rearranged to promote communication, connectedness and an integration of learning across different subject areas. Finally, teachers should be challenged to take a sideways step to view their classroom practice through new eyes and to become aware of themselves and their students as

---

32. See de Souza, 'Teaching for Effective Learning', *op cit*, and de Souza, 'Growing Empathetic, Compassionate, Meaningful and Hopefilled Students', *op cit*.

intuitive beings, thereby giving space and time to developing skills to access their inner lives which may lead to a greater sense of meaning, purpose and connectedness in their engagement with the outer world.

Contributors

Anthony J Kelly is a Redemptorist priest and former Chair of Theology at Australian Catholic University. Tony currently resides at the Brisbane Campus of ACU where he is Deputy Editor of *The Australian Journal of Theology* and a member of ACU's Graduate School of Philosophy and Theology.

Joyce Ann Mercer is an Associate Professor of Pastoral Theology at Virginia Theological Seminary and teaches in the pastoral theology programs. Joyce's publications include *Welcoming children: A Practical Theology of Childhood* and *Girl Talk, God Talk*.

Glen Cupit is a Senior Lecturer in Child Development at the DeLissa Institute of Early Childhood and Family Studies, University of South Australia where his principal responsibilities are to supervise and teach the program for honours students and to prepare all early childhood students for their role as practitioner researchers.

Jerome W Berryman is an Episcopal Priest at Christ Church Cathedral, Houston, Texas, where he researches the function of religious language in child development. Jerome developed Godly Play which teaches children the art of using religious language—parable, sacred story, silence and liturgical action - helping them become more fully aware of the mystery of God's presence in their lives.

Anne Hunt, is Rector of the Ballarat Campus, Australian Catholic University and a lecturer in systematic theology. She recently received and award for her book *Trinity: Nexus of the Mysteries of Christian Faith*.

Brendan Hyde is a member of the National School of Religious Education at Australian Catholic University in Melbourne. He is the author of a forthcoming (January 2008) book entitled

Children and Spirituality: Searching for Meaning and Connectedness, and co-author of forthcoming book (April 2008) *The Spiritual Dimension of Childhood.* Both will be published by Jessica Kingsley Publishers, London.

Marian de Souza is a Senior Lecturer in the School of Religious Education, Australian Catholic University, Ballarat campus and Editor of the Journal of Religious Education. Her teaching and research interests are in Spirituality and Education and she was the co-ordinating editor of *International handbook on the religious, moral and spiritual dimensions in education* published by Springer Academic publishers in 2006.

Winifred Wing Han Lamb is a high school teacher in Canberra and a Visiting Fellow in Philosophy at the School of Humanities, Australian National University, Canberra. She has published in the area of education and philosophy and is on the editorial board of *Interface.* Her recent book, *Living Truth and Truthful Living: Christian Faith and the Scalpel of Suspicion* is published by ATF Press.